55 Japanese Brunch Recipes for Home

By: Kelly Johnson

Table of Contents

- Tamagoyaki (Japanese Rolled Omelette)
- Okonomiyaki (Japanese Savory Pancake)
- Miso Soup with Tofu and Wakame
- Chawanmushi (Savory Egg Custard)
- Matcha Pancakes with Red Bean Paste
- Gyoza (Japanese Potstickers)
- Onigirazu (Sushi Sandwich)
- Nasu Dengaku (Miso-Glazed Eggplant)
- Japanese Souffle Pancakes
- Yudofu (Tofu Hot Pot)
- Saba Shioyaki (Grilled Mackerel)
- Tonkatsu (Japanese Pork Cutlet)
- Oyakodon (Chicken and Egg Rice Bowl)
- Shrimp and Vegetable Tempura
- Sakura Mochi (Cherry Blossom Rice Cake)
- Takikomi Gohan (Mixed Rice with Seasoned Ingredients)
- Katsu Sando (Japanese Cutlet Sandwich)
- Hijiki Salad with Soy Dressing
- Sake-Steamed Clams
- Zaru Soba (Cold Buckwheat Noodles)
- Hōtō (Japanese Thick Noodle Soup)
- Hiyayakko (Cold Tofu)
- Natto Toast with Avocado
- Kinoko Gohan (Mushroom Rice)
- Ebi Fry (Breaded and Fried Shrimp)
- Anmitsu (Japanese Fruit Jelly)
- Tori Soboro Don (Ground Chicken Rice Bowl)
- Yaki Udon (Stir-Fried Udon Noodles)
- Tofu Salad with Sesame Dressing
- Nikujaga (Japanese Meat and Potato Stew)
- Dorayaki (Red Bean Pancake Sandwich)
- Ochazuke (Rice with Tea)
- Chicken Teriyaki Bowl
- Hōrensō no Goma-ae (Spinach with Sesame Dressing)
- Kani Tamago Sushi (Crab and Egg Sushi)

- Ika Geso Karaage (Fried Squid Tentacles)
- Buta Kakuni (Braised Pork Belly)
- Yaki Imo (Roasted Sweet Potatoes)
- Atsuyaki Tamago (Thick Japanese Omelette)
- Yuba Salad (Tofu Skin Salad)
- Kakiage (Vegetable Tempura Fritters)
- Sake and Ikura Don (Salmon and Salmon Roe Rice Bowl)
- Hōtō Miso Soup
- Tofu Scramble with Vegetables
- Okara Korokke (Soy Pulp Croquettes)
- Tori Nanban Soba (Chicken Nanban Noodles)
- Chikuzenni (Simmered Chicken and Vegetables)
- Kuzumochi (Japanese Arrowroot Starch Cake)
- Sōmen Salad with Ponzu Dressing
- Yuzu Cheesecake
- Katsudon (Pork Cutlet and Egg Rice Bowl)
- Kappa Maki (Cucumber Sushi Roll)
- Saba Misoni (Mackerel Simmered in Miso)
- Daikon Radish Salad with Shiso Dressing
- Chazuke (Green Tea Rice Soup)

Tamagoyaki (Japanese Rolled Omelette)

Ingredients:

- 4 large eggs
- 2 tablespoons sugar
- 1/2 teaspoon soy sauce
- 1/2 teaspoon mirin (sweet rice wine)
- 1/4 teaspoon salt
- 1 tablespoon vegetable oil

Instructions:

Preparation:
- Crack the eggs into a bowl and whisk them well.
- Add sugar, soy sauce, mirin, and salt to the eggs. Mix until the sugar and salt are fully dissolved.

Cooking Tamagoyaki:
- Heat a rectangular tamagoyaki pan or a regular non-stick frying pan over medium heat. Brush the pan with vegetable oil.
- Pour a thin layer of the egg mixture into the pan, just enough to cover the bottom. Tilt the pan to spread the egg evenly.
- Once the bottom layer is set but still slightly runny on top, start rolling it from one end of the pan to the other using chopsticks or a spatula.
- Move the rolled egg to the far end of the pan, leaving space to pour more egg mixture. Add more mixture to cover the pan's bottom, including the rolled egg.
- When the new layer is set but still slightly runny, roll it up towards the already rolled egg. Repeat this process until all the egg mixture is used.

Shaping the Tamagoyaki:
- Once the tamagoyaki is fully cooked, shape it by pressing it down with the spatula to form a neat rectangular log.
- Transfer the rolled omelette to a bamboo sushi rolling mat, and while it's still warm, shape it tightly using the mat.

Serving:
- Let the tamagoyaki cool slightly before slicing it into bite-sized pieces.
- Serve the tamagoyaki slices as a side dish, in a bento box, or on top of sushi rice for tamago nigiri.

Optional Additions:
- For additional flavor and texture, you can add finely chopped scallions, cooked shrimp, or crab meat to the egg mixture.

Enjoy your homemade tamagoyaki – a delicious and slightly sweet Japanese rolled omelette!

Okonomiyaki (Japanese Savory Pancake)

Ingredients:

For the Batter:

- 2 cups all-purpose flour
- 1 1/2 cups dashi stock (Japanese fish and seaweed stock)
- 2 large eggs
- 1/2 medium cabbage, finely shredded
- 1/2 cup tenkasu (tempura scraps) or tempura batter bits
- 4 green onions, finely chopped
- 1/2 cup grated yamaimo (Japanese mountain yam), optional
- Salt and pepper to taste

For the Filling (Optional):

- Thinly sliced pork belly or cooked shrimp
- Beni shoga (pickled red ginger)
- Tenkasu (tempura scraps)

For Toppings:

- Okonomiyaki sauce (store-bought or homemade)
- Japanese mayonnaise
- Aonori (dried green seaweed flakes)
- Katsuobushi (bonito flakes)

Instructions:

Prepare the Batter:
- In a large bowl, whisk together the all-purpose flour and dashi stock until smooth.
- Add the eggs and continue whisking until well combined.
- Fold in the shredded cabbage, tenkasu or tempura bits, chopped green onions, grated yamaimo (if using), salt, and pepper. Mix well until the batter is evenly distributed.

Cooking Okonomiyaki:
- Heat a griddle or non-stick skillet over medium heat. Add a small amount of vegetable oil.
- Pour a portion of the batter onto the griddle, spreading it into a round pancake shape.
- If adding a filling, place slices of pork belly or cooked shrimp on top of the batter.
- Cook until the bottom is golden brown, then flip the okonomiyaki and cook the other side until golden and cooked through.

Toppings and Serving:
- Once cooked, transfer the okonomiyaki to a plate.
- Drizzle okonomiyaki sauce and Japanese mayonnaise over the top in a crisscross pattern.
- Sprinkle with aonori and katsuobushi.

Optional Toppings and Variations:
- Customize your okonomiyaki with additional toppings such as beni shoga (pickled red ginger) and extra tenkasu.

Serving Suggestions:
- Slice the okonomiyaki into wedges and serve it hot. You can also cut it into bite-sized pieces for sharing.

Enjoy your delicious homemade okonomiyaki – a delightful savory pancake that's both flavorful and satisfying!

Miso Soup with Tofu and Wakame

Ingredients:

- 4 cups dashi stock (Japanese fish and seaweed stock)
- 3 tablespoons miso paste (white or red miso)
- 1/2 cup tofu, diced into small cubes
- 2 tablespoons dried wakame seaweed, rehydrated
- 2 green onions, finely sliced
- 1 tablespoon soy sauce (optional, for additional flavor)
- Mirin (sweet rice wine) to taste (optional)
- 1 teaspoon sesame oil (optional, for extra richness)

Instructions:

Prepare Dashi Stock:
- In a pot, bring 4 cups of water to a simmer. Add dashi stock powder or bonito flakes and kombu (dried kelp). Simmer for about 5 minutes, then strain to obtain a clear dashi stock.

Rehydrate Wakame:
- Place the dried wakame seaweed in a bowl of water and let it soak for 5-10 minutes until it becomes tender. Drain and set aside.

Make Miso Base:
- In a small bowl, dissolve miso paste in a ladle or cup with a small amount of the dashi stock. Make sure there are no lumps.

Combine Ingredients:
- Return the strained dashi stock to the pot and bring it to a gentle simmer.
- Add the diced tofu to the simmering dashi stock. Let it cook for 2-3 minutes until the tofu is heated through.

Add Miso Paste:
- Lower the heat, and gradually add the dissolved miso paste to the soup, stirring gently. Avoid boiling the miso soup after adding miso to preserve its flavor.

Incorporate Wakame:
- Add the rehydrated wakame to the soup. Allow it to simmer for an additional 1-2 minutes.

Season and Garnish:
- Optionally, add soy sauce, mirin, or sesame oil to adjust the flavor to your liking.

- Garnish the miso soup with finely sliced green onions.

Serve:
- Ladle the miso soup into bowls and serve it hot.

Enjoy your comforting bowl of Miso Soup with Tofu and Wakame – a classic Japanese dish that's both nourishing and delicious!

Chawanmushi (Savory Egg Custard)

Ingredients:

For the Custard Base:

- 3 large eggs
- 2 cups dashi stock (Japanese fish and seaweed stock)
- 1 tablespoon soy sauce
- 1 tablespoon mirin (sweet rice wine)
- 1/2 teaspoon salt
- 1/2 teaspoon sugar

For Filling (Customizable):

- Cooked chicken pieces
- Shrimp, peeled and deveined
- Ginkgo nuts
- Shitake mushrooms, sliced
- Kamaboko (fish cake), sliced
- Snow peas, blanched
- Carrot, thinly sliced

Instructions:

Prepare Dashi Stock:
- In a pot, bring 2 cups of water to a simmer. Add dashi stock powder or bonito flakes and kombu (dried kelp). Simmer for about 5 minutes, then strain to obtain a clear dashi stock.

Prepare Custard Base:
- In a bowl, beat the eggs without creating too many bubbles.
- Gradually add the dashi stock, soy sauce, mirin, salt, and sugar. Mix well but avoid creating froth.

Assemble Custard Cups:
- Divide the chosen filling ingredients among individual chawanmushi cups or small heatproof bowls.

Pour Custard Mixture:
- Gently pour the egg custard mixture over the filling ingredients in each cup. Use a fine mesh strainer to remove any foam.

Steam Chawanmushi:
- Cover each cup with plastic wrap or aluminum foil to prevent water from dripping into the custard during steaming.
- Steam the chawanmushi cups in a steamer for approximately 15-20 minutes, or until the custard is set. The time may vary depending on the size of the cups.

Check for Doneness:
- To check if the chawanmushi is done, insert a toothpick into the center. If it comes out clean, the custard is cooked.

Serve:
- Carefully remove the cups from the steamer and serve the chawanmushi hot.

Garnish (Optional):
- Garnish with additional toppings like a sprinkle of chopped green onions or a drop of soy sauce if desired.

Enjoy your delicately steamed and savory Chawanmushi – a comforting and elegant Japanese dish!

Matcha Pancakes with Red Bean Paste

Ingredients:

For the Matcha Pancakes:

- 1 cup all-purpose flour
- 1 tablespoon matcha powder
- 2 tablespoons sugar
- 1 teaspoon baking powder
- 1/4 teaspoon salt
- 1 cup milk
- 1 large egg
- 2 tablespoons unsalted butter, melted
- 1 teaspoon vanilla extract

For the Red Bean Paste Filling:

- 1 cup sweetened red bean paste (canned or homemade)
- Water (as needed to adjust consistency)

Optional Toppings:

- Whipped cream
- Fresh berries
- Maple syrup

Instructions:

Make the Matcha Pancakes:

In a large bowl, whisk together the flour, matcha powder, sugar, baking powder, and salt.
In a separate bowl, whisk together the milk, egg, melted butter, and vanilla extract.
Pour the wet ingredients into the dry ingredients and gently stir until just combined. Do not overmix; it's okay if there are lumps.

Heat a griddle or non-stick skillet over medium heat. Lightly grease with butter or cooking spray.
Pour 1/4 cup of batter onto the griddle for each pancake. Cook until bubbles form on the surface, then flip and cook until the other side is golden brown.
Repeat until all the batter is used. Keep the cooked pancakes warm.

Prepare the Red Bean Paste Filling:

If the red bean paste is too thick, you can adjust the consistency by adding a small amount of water and mixing until smooth.

Assemble the Matcha Pancakes:

Take one pancake and spread a generous amount of red bean paste on top.
Place another pancake on top to create a sandwich, with the red bean paste in the middle.
Repeat for the desired number of pancake sandwiches.

Optional Toppings:

Top the pancake sandwiches with whipped cream, fresh berries, and a drizzle of maple syrup if desired.
Serve the Matcha Pancakes with Red Bean Paste warm and enjoy this delightful fusion of flavors!

These matcha pancakes with red bean paste make for a delicious and visually appealing breakfast or brunch treat.

Gyoza (Japanese Potstickers)

Ingredients:

For the Gyoza Filling:

- 1 pound ground pork
- 1 cup napa cabbage, finely chopped
- 2 cloves garlic, minced
- 1 tablespoon ginger, grated
- 2 green onions, finely chopped
- 2 tablespoons soy sauce
- 1 tablespoon sesame oil
- 1 teaspoon sugar
- 1/2 teaspoon salt
- 1/4 teaspoon black pepper

For the Gyoza Wrappers:

- Gyoza wrappers (store-bought or homemade)
- Water (for sealing wrappers)

For Dipping Sauce:

- 3 tablespoons soy sauce
- 1 tablespoon rice vinegar
- 1 teaspoon sesame oil
- 1 teaspoon sugar
- Red pepper flakes or chopped green onions (optional, for garnish)

Instructions:

Prepare the Gyoza Filling:

> In a large bowl, combine ground pork, chopped napa cabbage, minced garlic, grated ginger, chopped green onions, soy sauce, sesame oil, sugar, salt, and black pepper.
> Mix the ingredients thoroughly until well combined. You can use your hands or a spoon.

Assemble the Gyoza:

- Place a small amount of filling (about 1 teaspoon) in the center of a gyoza wrapper.
- Moisten the edges of the wrapper with water using your fingertip.
- Fold the wrapper in half, forming a half-moon shape, and press the edges to seal.
- You can leave the dumpling as is or create pleats along the edge for a decorative touch.
- Repeat the process until all the filling is used.

Cook the Gyoza:

- Heat a non-stick skillet with a lid over medium-high heat. Add a small amount of vegetable oil.
- Place the gyoza in the skillet, flat side down, and cook until the bottoms are golden brown.
- Add about 1/4 cup of water to the skillet and immediately cover with a lid. Steam the gyoza for 5-7 minutes or until the wrappers are translucent and the filling is cooked through.
- Remove the lid and let the gyoza continue cooking until the water evaporates and the bottoms crisp up again.
- Transfer the gyoza to a plate, crispy side down.

Prepare the Dipping Sauce:

- In a small bowl, mix together soy sauce, rice vinegar, sesame oil, and sugar.
- Adjust the proportions to taste. You can add red pepper flakes or chopped green onions for extra flavor.

Serve:

- Serve the gyoza hot with the dipping sauce on the side.
- Enjoy the delicious Japanese potstickers as an appetizer or part of a meal!

Feel free to customize the filling or adjust the dipping sauce according to your preferences.

Onigirazu (Sushi Sandwich)

Ingredients:

For the Sushi Rice:

- 2 cups sushi rice, cooked and seasoned with rice vinegar, sugar, and salt

For the Filling:

- Nori sheets (seaweed)
- Sliced cooked chicken, tuna, salmon, or your choice of protein
- Avocado slices
- Cucumber strips
- Shredded carrots
- Pickled ginger
- Soy sauce (for dipping)

Optional Sauces:

- Spicy mayo
- Teriyaki sauce

Instructions:

Prepare Sushi Rice:
- Cook sushi rice according to package instructions. Season the rice with rice vinegar, sugar, and salt. Allow it to cool to room temperature.

Assemble Onigirazu:
- Lay a sheet of plastic wrap on a clean surface.
- Place a sheet of nori on the plastic wrap, shiny side down.
- Spoon a portion of sushi rice onto the nori, spreading it evenly to cover the seaweed, leaving a border around the edges.

Add Filling:
- Arrange your desired fillings (sliced chicken, avocado, cucumber, shredded carrots, pickled ginger, etc.) on top of the rice.

Fold and Wrap:

- Fold the sides of the nori sheet over the filling to the center, creating a square shape.
- Fold the top and bottom of the nori over the filling, forming a neat package.
- Wrap the onigirazu tightly with the plastic wrap to secure it.

Repeat:
- Repeat the process to make more onigirazu with different fillings if desired.

Slice and Serve:
- Unwrap the plastic and slice the onigirazu in half using a sharp knife.
- Serve the onigirazu with soy sauce for dipping.

Optional Sauces:
- Drizzle with spicy mayo or teriyaki sauce for extra flavor.

Enjoy:
- Enjoy your onigirazu as a convenient and delicious sushi sandwich!

Onigirazu is versatile, and you can customize the fillings to suit your preferences. It's a great portable lunch option or a fun twist on traditional sushi.

Nasu Dengaku (Miso-Glazed Eggplant)

Ingredients:

- 2 medium-sized Japanese eggplants
- 2 tablespoons white miso paste
- 1 tablespoon mirin (sweet rice wine)
- 1 tablespoon sake (Japanese rice wine)
- 1 tablespoon sugar
- 1 tablespoon sesame oil
- Toasted sesame seeds and chopped green onions for garnish

Instructions:

Prepare the Eggplants:
- Preheat the oven broiler. Cut the eggplants in half lengthwise.
- Score the flesh of each eggplant half in a crisscross pattern, making sure not to cut through the skin.

Broil the Eggplants:
- Place the eggplant halves on a baking sheet, cut side up.
- Broil the eggplants for about 5-7 minutes or until the tops are charred and the flesh is tender. Keep an eye on them to prevent burning.

Make the Miso Glaze:
- In a small saucepan, combine miso paste, mirin, sake, sugar, and sesame oil.
- Heat the mixture over low heat, stirring continuously until the sugar dissolves and the glaze becomes smooth. Remove from heat.

Glaze the Eggplants:
- Brush the miso glaze generously over the cut side of each broiled eggplant half.

Broil Again:
- Return the eggplants to the broiler and broil for an additional 2-3 minutes, or until the miso glaze is bubbling and caramelized.

Garnish and Serve:
- Remove the eggplants from the oven and let them cool slightly.
- Garnish with toasted sesame seeds and chopped green onions.

Serve Warm:
- Serve the Nasu Dengaku warm as a side dish or appetizer.

Note: Nasu Dengaku can also be grilled on a barbecue or cooked on a stovetop grill pan for a smoky flavor.

Enjoy the rich and savory flavors of Nasu Dengaku – a classic Japanese dish that highlights the deliciousness of eggplant with a sweet and umami miso glaze!

Japanese Souffle Pancakes

Ingredients:

- 3 large eggs, separated
- 1/4 cup granulated sugar
- 1/4 cup whole milk
- 1/2 teaspoon vanilla extract
- 1/2 cup cake flour
- 1/2 teaspoon baking powder
- Pinch of salt
- Butter or oil for greasing the pan

Instructions:

Separate the Eggs:
- Carefully separate the egg yolks from the egg whites. Place them in two separate bowls.

Prepare the Batter:
- In the bowl with the egg yolks, add sugar and whisk until the mixture becomes pale and slightly thickened.
- Add milk and vanilla extract to the egg yolk mixture, and whisk until well combined.
- Sift in cake flour, baking powder, and a pinch of salt. Mix until just combined. Do not overmix.

Whip the Egg Whites:
- In the bowl with egg whites, use a clean, dry whisk or electric mixer to beat the egg whites until stiff peaks form.

Fold the Egg Whites:
- Gently fold the whipped egg whites into the batter in two or three additions. Be gentle to maintain the fluffiness.

Cooking the Pancakes:
- Heat a non-stick pan or griddle over low to medium heat. Grease with butter or oil.
- Spoon a portion of the batter onto the pan to create pancakes of your desired size. Keep the heat low to ensure the pancakes cook through without burning.

Cover and Cook:

- Cover the pan with a lid to help the pancakes cook through and rise. Cook for about 3-4 minutes on one side until the edges look set.

Flip and Cook Again:
- Carefully flip the pancakes using a spatula and cook for an additional 3-4 minutes on the other side, or until both sides are golden brown and the pancakes are cooked through.

Serve Immediately:
- Remove the pancakes from the pan and serve immediately while they are fluffy and light.

Optional Toppings:
- Top with maple syrup, fresh berries, whipped cream, or any other toppings of your choice.

Enjoy these delightful Japanese Soufflé Pancakes that are light, fluffy, and a perfect treat for breakfast or brunch!

Yudofu (Tofu Hot Pot)

Ingredients:

    Firm tofu: Use high-quality firm tofu, preferably silken tofu or momen tofu.
    Dashi (Japanese soup stock): You can use kombu (dried kelp) and katsuobushi (dried bonito flakes) to make dashi. Alternatively, you can use instant dashi granules or dashi stock concentrate.
    Soy sauce: For seasoning the broth.
    Mirin: A sweet rice wine that adds a subtle sweetness to the broth.
    Green onions: Sliced for garnish.
    Other optional ingredients: Mushrooms, napa cabbage, shiitake mushrooms, and other vegetables can be added for extra flavor and texture.

Instructions:

    Start by preparing the dashi. If using kombu and katsuobushi, soak the kombu in water for a few hours, then bring it to a gentle simmer. Add katsuobushi, let it simmer briefly, and strain the liquid.
    Cut the tofu into bite-sized cubes.
    In a pot, combine the dashi, soy sauce, and mirin. Bring the mixture to a simmer over medium heat.
    Gently add the tofu cubes to the simmering broth. Be careful not to break the tofu.
    Allow the tofu to simmer in the broth for about 10-15 minutes, allowing it to absorb the flavors of the broth.
    Add any additional vegetables you want to include, such as mushrooms or napa cabbage. Simmer until the vegetables are tender.
    Adjust the seasoning with soy sauce and mirin to taste.
    Serve the Yudofu in individual bowls, garnished with sliced green onions.

Yudofu is often enjoyed as a simple and comforting dish, especially during the colder months. It showcases the purity of tofu and the umami flavors of the dashi. Feel free to customize the recipe to your liking by adding your favorite vegetables or incorporating other ingredients.

Saba Shioyaki (Grilled Mackerel)

Ingredients:

    Mackerel fillets: Fresh mackerel is preferred, but you can also use frozen fillets.

Salt: For seasoning the mackerel.

Instructions:

Prepare the Mackerel:
- If using whole mackerel, clean and gut the fish or ask your fishmonger to do it for you. You can also purchase mackerel fillets if you prefer.
- Rinse the mackerel under cold water and pat it dry with paper towels.

Score the Mackerel:
- Use a sharp knife to make a few shallow diagonal cuts on both sides of the mackerel fillets. This helps the salt to penetrate and the fish to cook more evenly.

Season with Salt:
- Sprinkle a generous amount of salt on both sides of the mackerel fillets. Make sure to season the inside of the cuts you made as well.

Let it Rest:
- Allow the salted mackerel to rest for about 15-20 minutes. This helps the salt to permeate the fish and enhances the flavor.

Preheat the Grill:
- Preheat your grill to medium-high heat. If using an oven, preheat the broiler.

Grill the Mackerel:
- Place the mackerel fillets on the preheated grill or under the broiler. Grill each side for about 4-5 minutes, or until the skin is crispy and the fish is cooked through. Cooking time may vary depending on the thickness of the fillets.

Serve:
- Once the mackerel is cooked, transfer it to a serving plate. You can squeeze a bit of fresh lemon juice over the top if you like.

Garnish (Optional):
- Garnish with chopped green onions, grated daikon radish, or other toppings of your choice for added freshness and flavor.

Saba Shioyaki is often served with rice and miso soup, making for a satisfying and delicious meal. The simplicity of the preparation allows the natural flavors of the mackerel to shine through.

Tonkatsu (Japanese Pork Cutlet)

Ingredients:

Pork Loin or Pork Tenderloin: Choose boneless pork loin or tenderloin for this dish.
Salt and pepper: For seasoning the pork.
All-purpose flour: For dredging the pork.
Eggs: Beaten for coating the pork.
Panko breadcrumbs: Japanese-style breadcrumbs that provide a crispy texture.
Vegetable oil: For deep frying.

For Serving:

Tonkatsu sauce: A tangy and savory sauce specifically made for tonkatsu.
Shredded cabbage: Typically served on the side as a refreshing accompaniment.
Cooked rice: A common side dish.

Instructions:

Prepare the Pork:
- Trim excess fat from the pork loin or tenderloin and season with salt and pepper.

Dredge in Flour:
- Dredge the pork in all-purpose flour, shaking off any excess.

Coat in Beaten Eggs:
- Dip the floured pork into the beaten eggs, ensuring it's evenly coated.

Cover with Panko Breadcrumbs:
- Press the egg-coated pork into the panko breadcrumbs, making sure to coat the meat thoroughly. Press the breadcrumbs onto the pork to ensure a good adherence.

Repeat Coating (Optional):
- For an extra crispy coating, you can repeat the egg and panko coating process.

Heat Vegetable Oil:
- In a deep frying pan or pot, heat enough vegetable oil for deep frying to around 350-375°F (175-190°C).

Fry the Pork:

- Carefully place the breaded pork into the hot oil and fry until golden brown on both sides. This usually takes about 4-5 minutes per side, depending on the thickness of the pork.

Drain Excess Oil:
- Once cooked, place the tonkatsu on a wire rack or paper towels to drain excess oil.

Slice and Serve:
- Let the tonkatsu rest for a minute, then slice it into pieces. Serve it with shredded cabbage, rice, and tonkatsu sauce on the side.

Tonkatsu is a delicious and comforting dish with a crispy exterior and juicy interior. The combination of flavors and textures makes it a favorite in Japanese cuisine.

Oyakodon (Chicken and Egg Rice Bowl)

Ingredients:

Chicken thighs or breasts: Boneless and skinless, thinly sliced or cut into bite-sized pieces.
Onion: Thinly sliced.
Eggs: Lightly beaten.
Dashi (Japanese soup stock): You can use homemade dashi or dashi powder mixed with water.
Soy sauce: For seasoning.
Mirin: A sweet rice wine that adds sweetness to the broth.
Sugar: Optional, depending on your preference for sweetness.
Sake: Japanese rice wine, optional.
Green onions: Chopped for garnish.
Cooked rice: To serve the oyakodon.

Instructions:

Prepare Ingredients:
- Thinly slice the chicken and onion.
- Beat the eggs in a bowl.

Make the Broth:
- In a pan, combine the dashi, soy sauce, mirin, and sugar (if using). Bring it to a simmer over medium heat.

Cook Chicken and Onion:
- Add the sliced chicken and onions to the simmering broth. Cook until the chicken is cooked through and the onions are tender.

Add Beaten Eggs:
- Once the chicken is cooked, pour the beaten eggs evenly over the chicken and onions in the pan.

Simmer Gently:
- Allow the eggs to set slightly without stirring too much. The dish should have a slightly runny and custard-like consistency.

Finish Cooking:
- Once the eggs are cooked to your liking, remove the pan from heat. The residual heat will continue to cook the eggs.

Serve Over Rice:
- Spoon the chicken, onions, and eggs over a bowl of steamed rice.

Garnish and Serve:
- Garnish with chopped green onions and, if desired, drizzle a bit of sake over the top for extra flavor.

Oyakodon is typically served hot in a bowl, and the combination of savory broth, tender chicken, and creamy eggs over rice makes it a comforting and satisfying meal. Adjust the seasoning to your taste and enjoy this classic Japanese dish.

Shrimp and Vegetable Tempura

Ingredients:

For the Tempura Batter:

- 1 cup all-purpose flour
- 1 cup cornstarch
- 1 1/2 cups ice-cold water
- 1 egg, lightly beaten
- Ice cubes

For the Tempura:

- Shrimp, peeled and deveined (leave tails on)
- Assorted vegetables (e.g., sweet potatoes, bell peppers, zucchini, mushrooms, and broccoli), cut into bite-sized pieces
- Vegetable oil for deep-frying

For the Tentsuyu Dipping Sauce:

- 1 cup dashi (Japanese soup stock)
- 1/4 cup soy sauce
- 1/4 cup mirin (sweet rice wine)
- Optional: Grated daikon radish for serving

Instructions:

For the Tempura Batter:

> In a large mixing bowl, combine the all-purpose flour and cornstarch.
> Add the lightly beaten egg and ice-cold water to the dry ingredients. Mix gently until just combined. The batter should be lumpy, and it's important not to overmix.
> Place a handful of ice cubes in the batter to keep it cold.

For the Tempura:

> Heat vegetable oil in a deep fryer or a large, deep pan to 350-375°F (175-190°C).
> Dip the shrimp and vegetables into the tempura batter, ensuring they are well-coated.
> Carefully place the coated shrimp and vegetables into the hot oil. Fry in small batches to maintain the oil temperature.
> Fry until the tempura becomes golden and crispy, usually 2-3 minutes for vegetables and 3-4 minutes for shrimp.

Use a slotted spoon to remove the tempura from the oil and place them on a plate lined with paper towels to drain excess oil.

For the Tentsuyu Dipping Sauce:

In a small saucepan, combine the dashi, soy sauce, and mirin.
Bring the mixture to a simmer and let it cook for a couple of minutes.
Allow the dipping sauce to cool slightly before serving.

Serving:

Arrange the shrimp and vegetable tempura on a serving platter.
Serve with the tentsuyu dipping sauce.
Optionally, offer grated daikon radish as a condiment.

Enjoy your homemade shrimp and vegetable tempura with this light and crispy batter, complemented by the savory dipping sauce!

Sakura Mochi (Cherry Blossom Rice Cake)

Ingredients:

For the Mochi:

- 1 cup sweet rice (also known as glutinous rice or mochigome)
- 1 1/4 cups water
- A few drops of red food coloring (if making pink mochi)
- Cornstarch or potato starch for dusting

For the Filling:

- Sweet red bean paste (anko)

For the Cherry Blossom Leaves:

- Salted cherry blossom leaves (sakura leaves), available at Japanese grocery stores or online

Instructions:

For the Mochi:

Rinse the sweet rice under cold water until the water runs clear. Drain well. Combine the sweet rice with water in a rice cooker or on the stovetop. Cook the rice according to the package instructions.
While the rice is still warm, transfer it to a large bowl. Add a few drops of red food coloring if making pink mochi and mix well. Allow the colored rice to cool slightly.
Wet your hands with water and take a small portion of the colored rice. Flatten it in your palm and place a small amount of sweet red bean paste in the center.
Fold the rice over the filling to encase it, forming a small round or oval shape. Dust your hands with cornstarch or potato starch to prevent sticking and shape the mochi into a rounded or oval shape.

For the Cherry Blossom Leaves:

Rinse the salted cherry blossom leaves under cold water to remove excess salt. Gently pat the leaves dry with a paper towel.

Assembling:

Place a cherry blossom leaf on your work surface.

Put a mochi ball on top of the leaf and fold the leaf over the mochi.
Serve the Sakura Mochi with the cherry blossom leaf as an edible wrapper.

Sakura Mochi is often enjoyed as a delightful and symbolic treat during cherry blossom season in Japan. The combination of the chewy mochi, sweet red bean paste, and the fragrance of the cherry blossom leaves make it a unique and seasonal dessert.

Takikomi Gohan (Mixed Rice with Seasoned Ingredients)

Ingredients:

- 2 cups Japanese short-grain rice
- 2 1/4 cups dashi (Japanese soup stock)
- 2 tablespoons soy sauce
- 2 tablespoons sake (Japanese rice wine)
- 1 tablespoon mirin (sweet rice wine)
- 1 tablespoon vegetable oil
- 1 boneless, skinless chicken thigh, thinly sliced (optional)
- 1 carrot, julienned
- 1/2 cup sliced shiitake mushrooms
- 1/2 cup bamboo shoots, sliced (canned or fresh)
- 1/4 cup frozen green peas
- 2 green onions, thinly sliced
- Salt, to taste

Instructions:

Prepare the Rice:
- Rinse the rice under cold water until the water runs clear. Drain well.

Season the Ingredients:
- In a small bowl, mix together dashi, soy sauce, sake, and mirin to create the seasoning liquid.

Cooking:
- Heat vegetable oil in a pot or rice cooker.
- If using chicken, sauté the sliced chicken until browned.
- Add the julienned carrots, sliced shiitake mushrooms, and bamboo shoots. Sauté for a couple of minutes until the vegetables are slightly softened.

Add Rice and Seasoning Liquid:
- Add the rinsed and drained rice to the pot. Stir to coat the rice with the vegetables and meat.

Pour in the Seasoning Liquid:
- Pour the seasoning liquid over the rice and ingredients. Mix well.

Cooking:
- If using a pot, bring the mixture to a gentle boil. Reduce the heat to low, cover with a lid, and simmer for about 15-20 minutes, or until the rice is cooked and the liquid is absorbed.

- If using a rice cooker, transfer the mixture to the rice cooker and cook according to the rice cooker instructions.

Add Green Peas:
- In the last 5 minutes of cooking, add frozen green peas on top of the rice without stirring.

Finish and Garnish:
- Once the rice is cooked, fluff it gently with a fork, mixing in the green peas. Adjust the seasoning with salt if needed.
- Sprinkle sliced green onions on top for garnish.

Serve the Takikomi Gohan hot as a flavorful and wholesome one-pot meal. The combination of seasoned ingredients infuses the rice with delicious flavors, making it a satisfying and comforting dish.

Katsu Sando (Japanese Cutlet Sandwich)

Ingredients:

For the Cutlet:

- Pork or chicken cutlets (thinly pounded)
- Salt and pepper, to taste
- All-purpose flour, for dredging
- Eggs, beaten
- Panko breadcrumbs

For the Sandwich:

- Soft, white bread slices
- Tonkatsu sauce (store-bought or homemade)
- Shredded cabbage (optional)
- Japanese mayonnaise (optional)

Instructions:

For the Cutlet:

Season the pork or chicken cutlets with salt and pepper on both sides.
Dredge each cutlet in all-purpose flour, shaking off any excess.
Dip the floured cutlets into beaten eggs, ensuring they are well-coated.
Coat the cutlets with Panko breadcrumbs, pressing the breadcrumbs onto the meat to adhere.
Heat vegetable oil in a pan over medium heat. Fry the cutlets until they are golden brown and cooked through, about 3-4 minutes per side. Place them on a paper towel to drain excess oil.

Assembling the Sandwich:

Toast the slices of white bread lightly if desired.
Spread tonkatsu sauce on one side of each slice of bread.
Place a fried cutlet on one slice of bread.
If using shredded cabbage, place a layer on top of the cutlet.
Optionally, add a drizzle of Japanese mayonnaise.
Top with the second slice of bread, tonkatsu sauce side down.
Repeat the process for additional sandwiches.
Use a sharp knife to cut the sandwich in half diagonally.

Serve the Katsu Sando immediately, and enjoy the crispy, flavorful cutlet sandwiched between soft bread slices. It's a popular and satisfying Japanese sandwich that combines contrasting textures and savory flavors.

Hijiki Salad with Soy Dressing

Ingredients:

For the Salad:

- 1/2 cup dried hijiki seaweed
- 1 cup water (for soaking hijiki)
- 1 tablespoon vegetable oil
- 1 carrot, julienned
- 1/2 cup shelled edamame (cooked and cooled)
- 1/4 cup sliced or julienned cucumber
- 2 tablespoons toasted sesame seeds (optional)

For the Soy Dressing:

- 2 tablespoons soy sauce
- 1 tablespoon rice vinegar
- 1 tablespoon mirin (sweet rice wine)
- 1 teaspoon sugar
- 1 teaspoon sesame oil
- 1 teaspoon grated ginger

Instructions:

For the Hijiki Salad:

Soak the Hijiki:
- Place the dried hijiki in a bowl and cover it with 1 cup of water. Allow it to soak for about 20-30 minutes or until the hijiki becomes rehydrated.

Prepare the Vegetables:
- Julienne the carrot and cucumber.
- If not already cooked, cook the edamame according to the package instructions. Cool them down.

Cook the Hijiki:
- Heat vegetable oil in a pan over medium heat. Drain the soaked hijiki and sauté it in the pan for 2-3 minutes.

Assemble the Salad:
- In a mixing bowl, combine the sautéed hijiki, julienned carrot, cooked edamame, sliced cucumber, and toasted sesame seeds (if using).

For the Soy Dressing:

Prepare the Dressing:
- In a small bowl, whisk together soy sauce, rice vinegar, mirin, sugar, sesame oil, and grated ginger until well combined.

Dress the Salad:
- Pour the soy dressing over the hijiki salad and toss gently to coat all the ingredients evenly.

Chill (Optional):
- If you prefer a chilled salad, refrigerate it for about 30 minutes before serving.

Serve:
- Serve the Hijiki Salad in individual bowls or as a side dish.

Enjoy this nutritious and flavorful Hijiki Salad with Soy Dressing as a refreshing and healthy addition to your Japanese-inspired meals. The combination of hijiki seaweed with the crisp vegetables and umami-packed soy dressing creates a delightful dish.

Sake-Steamed Clams

Ingredients:

- 2 pounds fresh clams (Asari clams or littleneck clams)
- 1/2 cup sake
- 2 cloves garlic, minced
- 1 tablespoon soy sauce
- 1 tablespoon mirin (sweet rice wine)
- 1 tablespoon sesame oil (optional)
- Green onions, chopped (for garnish)
- Red chili flakes (optional, for added spice)

Instructions:

Clean the Clams:
- Scrub the clam shells under cold running water to remove any sand or debris. Discard any clams with cracked or open shells that do not close when tapped.

Prepare the Broth:
- In a large pot or deep sauté pan, combine the sake, minced garlic, soy sauce, mirin, and sesame oil (if using). Stir to mix the ingredients.

Steam the Clams:
- Add the cleaned clams to the pot, ensuring they are in a single layer.
- Cover the pot with a lid and steam the clams over medium-high heat for 5-7 minutes, or until the clams have opened. Discard any clams that do not open.

Garnish and Serve:
- Once the clams have opened, transfer them to serving bowls.
- Pour the steaming broth over the clams.
- Garnish with chopped green onions and, if desired, a sprinkle of red chili flakes for added spice.

Serve Immediately:
- Serve the sake-steamed clams immediately while they are hot. You can serve them as an appetizer or as part of a larger seafood meal.

Enjoy the delicate and briny flavor of the sake-steamed clams, complemented by the aromatic broth. Serve the dish with some crusty bread or steamed rice to soak up the delicious broth. It's a delightful and easy-to-make dish that highlights the natural flavors of fresh clams.

Zaru Soba (Cold Buckwheat Noodles)

Ingredients:

For the Soba Noodles:

- 8 ounces (about 230 grams) soba noodles
- Water for boiling
- Ice water for rinsing

For the Dipping Sauce (Tsuyu):

- 1/2 cup soy sauce
- 1/4 cup mirin (sweet rice wine)
- 1/4 cup sake (Japanese rice wine)
- 1 tablespoon sugar
- 1 cup dashi (Japanese soup stock)
- Optional toppings: sliced green onions, wasabi, shredded nori seaweed, grated daikon radish

Instructions:

Cooking and Rinsing the Soba Noodles:

Cook the Soba Noodles:
- Bring a large pot of water to a boil.
- Add soba noodles and cook according to the package instructions (usually about 5-8 minutes), stirring occasionally to prevent sticking.
- Drain the noodles and rinse them thoroughly under cold running water to remove excess starch and cool them down quickly.

Prepare Ice Water:
- Fill a large bowl with ice water. Place the rinsed soba noodles in the ice water to chill. This helps maintain a firm texture and stops the cooking process.

Drain and Arrange the Noodles:
- Drain the soba noodles again and arrange them on a bamboo or mesh sieve (zaru) to allow any remaining water to drip off.

Making the Dipping Sauce (Tsuyu):

Combine Ingredients:
- In a bowl, mix together soy sauce, mirin, sake, sugar, and dashi. Stir until the sugar is dissolved.

Chill (Optional):

- If you prefer a colder dipping sauce, you can refrigerate it for a short time before serving.

Serving:

Individual Servings:
- Divide the chilled soba noodles into individual portions and place them on small plates or bamboo mats.

Toppings:
- Optionally, sprinkle sliced green onions and shredded nori over the noodles. Serve with wasabi and grated daikon radish on the side.

Dipping Sauce:
- Pour a portion of the tsuyu dipping sauce into individual small bowls for each person.

Enjoy:
- To eat, take a portion of the cold soba noodles, dip them into the tsuyu sauce, and savor the refreshing flavors.

Zaru Soba is a light and flavorful dish that makes for a perfect summer meal. The combination of the chilled buckwheat noodles with the savory and slightly sweet dipping sauce creates a delightful and satisfying experience.

Hōtō (Japanese Thick Noodle Soup)

Ingredients:

For the Soup:

- 8 cups dashi (Japanese soup stock)
- 3 tablespoons miso paste (white or red miso)
- 2 tablespoons soy sauce
- 1 tablespoon mirin (sweet rice wine)
- 1 tablespoon sake (Japanese rice wine)
- 1 tablespoon vegetable oil
- 1 onion, sliced
- 2 carrots, sliced
- 1 leek, sliced
- 1 potato, peeled and diced
- 1/2 kabocha squash, peeled, seeds removed, and diced
- 8 ounces (about 230 grams) hōtō noodles or udon noodles

For Serving:

- Green onions, chopped (for garnish)
- Shichimi togarashi (Japanese seven-spice blend) or black pepper
- Toasted sesame seeds (optional)

Instructions:

Prepare Vegetables:
- Slice the onion, carrots, leek, and peel and dice the potato and kabocha squash.

Cooking the Soup Base:
- In a large pot, heat vegetable oil over medium heat. Add sliced onion and cook until softened.
- Add the sliced leek, carrots, potato, and kabocha squash to the pot. Sauté for a few minutes until the vegetables start to become tender.

Make the Broth:
- Pour dashi into the pot with the sautéed vegetables. Bring it to a simmer.
- In a small bowl, mix miso paste with a few tablespoons of hot broth to dissolve it. Add the miso mixture back into the pot.

- Add soy sauce, mirin, and sake to the broth. Stir well and let it simmer until all the vegetables are cooked through.

Cook the Noodles:
- Meanwhile, cook the hōtō noodles or udon noodles according to the package instructions. Drain and set aside.

Assemble the Soup:
- Once the vegetables are tender, add the cooked noodles to the pot. Stir gently to combine.

Serve:
- Ladle the hōtō soup into bowls. Garnish with chopped green onions, sprinkle with shichimi togarashi or black pepper, and optionally add toasted sesame seeds.

Hōtō is a comforting and nourishing noodle soup with a rich miso-based broth and hearty vegetables. It's perfect for colder weather and a delightful way to enjoy Japanese flavors.

Hiyayakko (Cold Tofu)

Ingredients:

- Silken or soft tofu (1 block)
- Soy sauce
- Ponzu sauce (a citrus-flavored soy-based sauce)
- Grated ginger
- Finely chopped green onions
- Sesame seeds (optional)
- Shredded nori seaweed (optional)

Instructions:

   Prepare the Tofu:
   - Remove the tofu from its packaging and drain any excess water.
   - Gently transfer the tofu block to a serving plate without breaking it.

   Cut the Tofu:
   - Cut the tofu into individual serving portions. This is typically done into cubes or rectangles, depending on your preference.

   Add Toppings:
   - Sprinkle grated ginger over the tofu. The amount can be adjusted based on your taste preferences.
   - Add finely chopped green onions on top of the tofu.

   Soy Sauce and Ponzu Sauce:
   - Drizzle a small amount of soy sauce over each piece of tofu.
   - Pour a bit of ponzu sauce over the tofu. Ponzu adds a citrusy and tangy flavor.

   Optional Toppings:
   - Optionally, sprinkle sesame seeds and shredded nori seaweed for added texture and flavor.

   Serve Cold:
   - Hiyayakko is meant to be served cold, so you can refrigerate the tofu before serving if you'd like it extra chilled.

   Enjoy:
   - Serve the Hiyayakko immediately and enjoy the cool, silky texture of the tofu with the flavorful toppings.

Hiyayakko is a versatile dish, and you can customize it with additional toppings such as bonito flakes, grated daikon radish, or even a drizzle of sesame oil. It's a light and healthy option that showcases the natural taste of tofu while offering a burst of flavors from the toppings and sauces.

Natto Toast with Avocado

Ingredients:

- 2 slices of your favorite bread (whole grain, sourdough, or any preferred type)
- 1 package of natto (fermented soybeans)
- 1 ripe avocado
- Soy sauce (optional, for seasoning natto)
- Toasted sesame seeds (optional, for garnish)
- Nori seaweed, shredded (optional, for garnish)
- Red pepper flakes (optional, for a bit of heat)

Instructions:

Toast the Bread:
- Toast the slices of bread to your desired level of crispiness.

Prepare the Natto:
- Open the package of natto and follow the instructions provided. Typically, you'll find a small packet of soy sauce and mustard within the natto package. Mix the natto well to create a sticky and stringy consistency. Add soy sauce to taste, if desired.

Mash the Avocado:
- While the bread is toasting and the natto is being prepared, cut the ripe avocado in half, remove the pit, and scoop the flesh into a bowl. Mash the avocado with a fork until it reaches your desired consistency.

Assemble the Toast:
- Once the bread is toasted, spread the mashed avocado evenly on each slice.
- Spoon the prepared natto on top of the avocado. The combination of creamy avocado and sticky natto creates a unique and delicious texture.

Garnish (Optional):
- Sprinkle toasted sesame seeds, shredded nori seaweed, and red pepper flakes on top for added flavor and presentation.

Serve:
- Natto toast with avocado can be enjoyed for breakfast, brunch, or as a satisfying snack. It's a flavorful and nutrient-packed dish that showcases the umami of natto and the creaminess of avocado.

Feel free to customize this recipe based on your preferences. The combination of natto and avocado provides a good balance of textures and flavors, making it a nutritious and satisfying option for a quick and easy meal.

Kinoko Gohan (Mushroom Rice)

Ingredients:

- 2 cups Japanese short-grain rice
- 1 1/2 cups assorted mushrooms (shiitake, shimeji, enoki, maitake, etc.), cleaned and sliced
- 1 3/4 cups dashi (Japanese soup stock)
- 2 tablespoons soy sauce
- 1 tablespoon sake (Japanese rice wine)
- 1 tablespoon mirin (sweet rice wine)
- 1 tablespoon vegetable oil
- 1 green onion, thinly sliced (for garnish)
- Sesame seeds (for garnish, optional)

Instructions:

Rinse the Rice:
- Rinse the rice under cold water until the water runs clear. Drain well.

Prepare the Mushrooms:
- Clean and slice the assorted mushrooms. If using shiitake mushrooms, remove the stems and slice the caps.

Cook the Mushrooms:
- Heat vegetable oil in a pot or rice cooker. Add the sliced mushrooms and sauté until they are lightly browned.

Add Rice and Seasonings:
- Add the rinsed rice to the pot with the mushrooms. Stir to coat the rice in the oil and mushrooms.
- In a separate bowl, mix together dashi, soy sauce, sake, and mirin. Pour this mixture over the rice and mushrooms.

Cook the Rice:
- If using a pot, bring the mixture to a simmer, then reduce the heat to low, cover with a lid, and cook for about 15-20 minutes or until the rice is cooked and the liquid is absorbed.
- If using a rice cooker, transfer the rice and mushroom mixture to the rice cooker and cook according to the rice cooker instructions.

Fluff the Rice:
- Once the rice is cooked, fluff it gently with a fork to distribute the mushrooms evenly.

Garnish and Serve:

- Garnish the Kinoko Gohan with sliced green onions and, if desired, sesame seeds.

Serve Warm:
- Kinoko Gohan is traditionally served warm as a side dish or as a standalone dish.

This Mushroom Rice is a delightful and earthy dish that showcases the rich flavors of various mushrooms. It pairs well with a variety of Japanese meals and can be enjoyed on its own for a comforting and satisfying experience.

Ebi Fry (Breaded and Fried Shrimp)

Ingredients:

- 12 large shrimp, peeled and deveined
- Salt and pepper, to taste
- 1/2 cup all-purpose flour
- 2 large eggs, beaten
- 1 cup Panko breadcrumbs
- Vegetable oil, for frying
- Tonkatsu sauce, for serving
- Lemon wedges, for garnish (optional)

Instructions:

Prepare the Shrimp:
- Peel and devein the shrimp, leaving the tails intact. Make shallow cuts on the inner side of each shrimp to prevent them from curling during frying. Pat them dry with paper towels.

Season the Shrimp:
- Season the shrimp with salt and pepper on both sides.

Coat in Flour:
- Dredge each shrimp in all-purpose flour, shaking off excess flour.

Dip in Egg:
- Dip the floured shrimp into the beaten eggs, ensuring they are well-coated.

Coat in Panko Breadcrumbs:
- Roll the egg-coated shrimp in Panko breadcrumbs, pressing the breadcrumbs onto the shrimp to adhere.

Heat the Oil:
- In a deep pan or skillet, heat enough vegetable oil for frying to 350-375°F (175-190°C).

Fry the Shrimp:
- Carefully place the breaded shrimp into the hot oil in batches, ensuring not to overcrowd the pan. Fry until they turn golden brown, usually 2-3 minutes per side.

Drain Excess Oil:
- Use a slotted spoon to remove the fried shrimp from the oil and place them on a plate lined with paper towels to drain excess oil.

Serve:

- Arrange the Ebi Fry on a serving plate. Serve with tonkatsu sauce for dipping and optionally garnish with lemon wedges.

Enjoy:
- Ebi Fry is best enjoyed immediately while the coating is crispy. Dip the shrimp in tonkatsu sauce or your favorite dipping sauce.

Ebi Fry makes for a delightful appetizer or main course. The combination of the crispy outer layer and tender shrimp inside is a crowd-pleaser. Serve it with a side of rice, shredded cabbage, or a simple salad for a complete meal.

Anmitsu (Japanese Fruit Jelly)

Ingredients:

For the Agar Jelly:

- 4 cups water
- 2 teaspoons agar or kanten powder
- 1/2 cup sugar

For the Mitsumame (Sweet Syrup):

- 1 cup water
- 1/2 cup sugar
- 2 tablespoons Mizuame (Japanese sweetener) or corn syrup

Additional Ingredients:

- Sweet azuki (red bean paste)
- Assorted fruits (canned or fresh), such as peaches, pineapple, strawberries, and oranges, cut into bite-sized pieces
- Shiratama dango (sweet rice dumplings) - optional
- Vanilla ice cream - optional

Instructions:

For the Agar Jelly:

    Prepare the Agar Mixture:
- In a saucepan, combine water, agar or kanten powder, and sugar. Stir well to dissolve the sugar.

    Boil the Mixture:
- Bring the mixture to a boil over medium heat, stirring continuously. Once it boils, reduce the heat and simmer for 2-3 minutes until the agar or kanten is fully dissolved.

    Cool and Set:
- Remove the saucepan from the heat and let the mixture cool slightly. Pour it into a mold or shallow dish and let it set in the refrigerator for a few hours or until firm.

    Cut into Cubes:
- Once set, cut the agar jelly into small cubes.

For the Mitsumame (Sweet Syrup):

Prepare the Sweet Syrup:
- In a separate saucepan, combine water, sugar, and Mizuame or corn syrup. Bring it to a boil, stirring to dissolve the sugar.

Cool the Syrup:
- Remove the syrup from the heat and let it cool. You can chill it in the refrigerator if desired.

Assembling Anmitsu:

Assemble the Components:
- Place a few cubes of agar jelly in serving bowls.
- Add a dollop of sweet azuki (red bean paste) on top of the jelly cubes.
- Arrange assorted fruits around the jelly and red bean paste.
- Optionally, add shiratama dango (sweet rice dumplings) and a scoop of vanilla ice cream.

Drizzle with Sweet Syrup:
- Pour the cooled Mitsumame syrup over the arranged ingredients.

Serve:
- Serve Anmitsu chilled and enjoy the delightful combination of textures and flavors.

Anmitsu is a visually appealing and refreshing dessert, perfect for hot weather. The combination of the sweet syrup, chewy agar jelly, red bean paste, and fresh fruits creates a delightful treat with a variety of textures and flavors.

Tori Soboro Don (Ground Chicken Rice Bowl)

Ingredients:

For the Tori Soboro (Ground Chicken):

- 1 lb ground chicken
- 2 tablespoons soy sauce
- 2 tablespoons mirin (sweet rice wine)
- 1 tablespoon sake (Japanese rice wine)
- 1 tablespoon sugar
- 1 tablespoon vegetable oil
- 2 green onions, finely chopped (for garnish)

For the Rice Bowl:

- Steamed Japanese short-grain rice (enough for serving)
- Nori seaweed, shredded (optional, for garnish)
- Pickled red ginger (beni shoga, optional, for garnish)
- Sesame seeds (optional, for garnish)
- Steamed or blanched vegetables (optional, for serving)

Instructions:

For the Tori Soboro (Ground Chicken):

Cook Ground Chicken:
- Heat vegetable oil in a pan over medium heat. Add the ground chicken and cook, breaking it apart with a spatula, until it is no longer pink.

Season the Chicken:
- Add soy sauce, mirin, sake, and sugar to the cooked chicken. Continue cooking and stirring until the liquid is mostly absorbed, and the chicken becomes slightly caramelized.

Finish Cooking:
- Cook until the ground chicken is cooked through and has a slightly sticky texture. Remove from heat.

Garnish:
- Stir in chopped green onions and set aside.

For Assembling Tori Soboro Don:

Prepare Rice:

- Serve a portion of steamed Japanese short-grain rice in a bowl.

Top with Tori Soboro:
- Spoon the seasoned ground chicken (Tori Soboro) over the rice.

Garnish:
- Garnish with shredded nori seaweed, pickled red ginger, sesame seeds, and any additional toppings you prefer.

Optional Vegetables:
- You can add steamed or blanched vegetables of your choice, such as spinach, broccoli, or snow peas, to the bowl for added color and nutrition.

Serve:
- Serve Tori Soboro Don hot and enjoy the delicious combination of seasoned ground chicken over steamed rice.

Tori Soboro Don is a versatile dish, and you can customize it based on your preferences. The sweet and savory flavor of the ground chicken pairs well with the simplicity of steamed rice, creating a satisfying and comforting meal.

Yaki Udon (Stir-Fried Udon Noodles)

Ingredients:

- 8 ounces (about 230 grams) udon noodles
- 2 tablespoons vegetable oil
- 1/2 pound (about 225 grams) protein of your choice (sliced chicken, beef, pork, shrimp, or tofu)
- 1 onion, thinly sliced
- 1 carrot, julienned
- 1 bell pepper, thinly sliced
- 2 cups cabbage, thinly sliced
- 2 green onions, sliced diagonally (for garnish)

For the Sauce:

- 3 tablespoons soy sauce
- 2 tablespoons oyster sauce
- 1 tablespoon mirin (sweet rice wine)
- 1 tablespoon sake (Japanese rice wine)
- 1 teaspoon sugar
- 1 teaspoon sesame oil

Instructions:

Cook the Udon Noodles:
- Cook the udon noodles according to the package instructions. Once cooked, drain and rinse them under cold water to stop the cooking process. Set aside.

Prepare the Sauce:
- In a small bowl, whisk together soy sauce, oyster sauce, mirin, sake, sugar, and sesame oil to create the sauce. Set aside.

Stir-Fry the Protein:
- Heat 1 tablespoon of vegetable oil in a large pan or wok over medium-high heat. Add the sliced protein (chicken, beef, pork, shrimp, or tofu) and stir-fry until cooked through. Remove the cooked protein from the pan and set aside.

Stir-Fry Vegetables:

- In the same pan, add another tablespoon of vegetable oil. Add the sliced onion, julienned carrot, sliced bell pepper, and shredded cabbage. Stir-fry until the vegetables are tender but still crisp.

Combine Noodles and Sauce:
- Add the cooked udon noodles to the pan with the stir-fried vegetables. Pour the prepared sauce over the noodles and vegetables.

Stir-Fry Together:
- Toss everything together, ensuring that the noodles and vegetables are well coated with the sauce. Cook for a few more minutes until everything is heated through.

Add Protein:
- Return the cooked protein to the pan and toss to combine with the noodles and vegetables. Cook for an additional 2-3 minutes.

Garnish and Serve:
- Garnish the Yaki Udon with sliced green onions. Serve hot and enjoy.

Yaki Udon is a versatile dish, and you can customize it with your favorite vegetables and protein. It's a delicious and satisfying stir-fried noodle dish that is quick and easy to prepare at home.

Tofu Salad with Sesame Dressing

Ingredients:

For the Salad:

- 1 block (about 14 ounces) firm tofu, drained and cubed
- 1 cucumber, julienned
- 1 carrot, julienned
- 1 cup cherry tomatoes, halved
- Mixed salad greens (lettuce, spinach, arugula, etc.)

For the Sesame Dressing:

- 2 tablespoons sesame paste or tahini
- 2 tablespoons soy sauce
- 1 tablespoon rice vinegar
- 1 tablespoon mirin (sweet rice wine)
- 1 tablespoon sesame oil
- 1 teaspoon sugar
- 1 clove garlic, minced (optional)
- 1 teaspoon grated ginger

Optional Toppings:

- Toasted sesame seeds
- Chopped green onions
- Crispy fried shallots or garlic

Instructions:

For the Sesame Dressing:

   Prepare the Dressing:
   - In a bowl, whisk together sesame paste or tahini, soy sauce, rice vinegar, mirin, sesame oil, sugar, minced garlic (optional), and grated ginger until well combined. Adjust the sweetness and saltiness according to your taste.

For the Tofu Salad:

   Prepare the Tofu:

- Drain the firm tofu and cut it into bite-sized cubes.

Prepare the Vegetables:
- Julienne the cucumber and carrot. Halve the cherry tomatoes. Wash and prepare the mixed salad greens.

Assemble the Salad:
- In a large salad bowl, combine the cubed tofu, julienned cucumber, julienned carrot, cherry tomatoes, and mixed salad greens.

Toss with Sesame Dressing:
- Drizzle the sesame dressing over the salad and gently toss until all the ingredients are well coated with the dressing.

Optional Toppings:
- Sprinkle toasted sesame seeds, chopped green onions, and crispy fried shallots or garlic on top for added flavor and texture.

Serve:
- Serve the Tofu Salad with Sesame Dressing immediately as a refreshing and nutritious side dish or a light meal.

This Tofu Salad with Sesame Dressing is a delightful combination of textures and flavors. The creamy tofu pairs well with the crisp vegetables, and the sesame dressing adds a nutty and savory kick. It's a versatile salad that can be enjoyed on its own or as a complement to a variety of main dishes.

Nikujaga (Japanese Meat and Potato Stew)

Ingredients:

- 1 lb thinly sliced beef (such as sukiyaki or shabu-shabu beef)
- 4 medium potatoes, peeled and cut into bite-sized chunks
- 2 carrots, peeled and sliced into rounds
- 1 onion, thinly sliced
- 1 cup green beans, trimmed and cut into bite-sized pieces
- 1 cup shirataki noodles (optional), rinsed and drained
- 4 cups dashi (Japanese soup stock)
- 1/3 cup soy sauce
- 1/4 cup mirin (sweet rice wine)
- 2 tablespoons sugar
- 1 tablespoon sake (Japanese rice wine)
- 2 tablespoons vegetable oil
- Green onions, chopped (for garnish)

Instructions:

Prepare Vegetables:
- Peel and cut the potatoes into bite-sized chunks. Slice the carrots, thinly slice the onion, and cut the green beans into bite-sized pieces.

Cook Shirataki Noodles (if using):
- If using shirataki noodles, rinse them under cold water and drain.

Cooking the Vegetables:
- In a large pot or a deep pan, heat vegetable oil over medium heat. Add the thinly sliced onion and cook until softened.
- Add the sliced beef to the pot and cook until the beef is browned.

Add Potatoes and Carrots:
- Add the potatoes and carrots to the pot, followed by the shirataki noodles if using.

Prepare the Broth:
- In a bowl, mix together dashi, soy sauce, mirin, sugar, and sake. Pour this broth mixture over the vegetables and beef in the pot.

Simmer:
- Bring the mixture to a boil, then reduce the heat to low, cover with a lid, and simmer for about 20-30 minutes or until the potatoes are tender.

Add Green Beans:

- Add the green beans to the pot and simmer for an additional 5-7 minutes until the green beans are cooked but still crisp.

Adjust Seasoning:
- Adjust the seasoning if needed by adding more soy sauce, mirin, or sugar according to your taste.

Serve:
- Once the vegetables are tender and the flavors have melded, serve Nikujaga in bowls. Garnish with chopped green onions.

Nikujaga is often served with a bowl of steamed rice, making it a comforting and satisfying meal. This hearty stew showcases the comforting combination of tender beef, flavorful broth, and hearty vegetables.

Dorayaki (Red Bean Pancake Sandwich)

Ingredients:

For the Pancakes:

- 2 large eggs
- 1/2 cup sugar
- 1 tablespoon honey or mirin
- 1 cup all-purpose flour
- 1 teaspoon baking powder
- 1 tablespoon water

For the Filling:

- Sweet red bean paste (anko), homemade or store-bought

Instructions:

For the Pancakes:

Prepare the Batter:
- In a mixing bowl, whisk together eggs and sugar until well combined and slightly fluffy.

Add Honey or Mirin:
- Add honey or mirin to the egg and sugar mixture and mix well.

Sift Dry Ingredients:
- Sift together the all-purpose flour and baking powder. Gradually add the dry ingredients to the wet ingredients, mixing to form a smooth batter.

Add Water:
- Add water to the batter and mix until smooth. The batter should be thick but pourable.

Rest the Batter:
- Allow the batter to rest for about 15-20 minutes. This helps the pancakes become fluffier.

Cooking the Pancakes:
- Heat a non-stick pan or griddle over medium-low heat. Lightly grease the surface with a small amount of oil or butter.
- Pour small circles of batter onto the pan, keeping them about 3 inches in diameter. Cook until bubbles form on the surface, then flip and cook the other side until golden brown.

- Repeat until all the batter is used. Keep the cooked pancakes covered to retain moisture.

Assembling Dorayaki:

Cool the Pancakes:
- Allow the pancakes to cool completely before assembling the Dorayaki.

Spread Red Bean Paste:
- Take one pancake and spread a layer of sweet red bean paste (anko) over the entire surface.

Sandwich with Another Pancake:
- Place another pancake on top, creating a sandwich with the red bean paste in the middle.

Press Gently:
- Press the pancakes gently together to secure the filling.

Repeat:
- Repeat the process for the remaining pancakes.

Serve:
- Dorayaki can be served at room temperature and enjoyed as a delicious snack or dessert.

Dorayaki is a beloved treat in Japan, and its delightful combination of fluffy pancakes and sweet red bean paste makes it a favorite among both children and adults. You can experiment with different fillings or even try making your own homemade red bean paste for a personalized touch.

Ochazuke (Rice with Tea)

Ingredients:

- Cooked Japanese short-grain rice
- Green tea or dashi (Japanese soup stock)
- Toppings of your choice (see suggestions below)
- Soy sauce
- Wasabi (optional)
- Nori seaweed, shredded (optional)

Topping Suggestions:

- Grilled salmon or smoked salmon, flaked
- Pickled plums (umeboshi), chopped
- Seaweed (nori) strips
- Sesame seeds
- Shredded nori seaweed
- Thinly sliced green onions
- Shiso leaves, chopped
- Furikake (Japanese rice seasoning)

Instructions:

Prepare Toppings:
- Prepare your desired toppings. This can include flaked grilled or smoked salmon, chopped pickled plums, seaweed strips, sesame seeds, green onions, shiso leaves, or furikake.

Brew Green Tea or Dashi:
- Brew a cup of green tea or prepare a cup of dashi. The choice between green tea and dashi depends on your preference.

Assemble Ochazuke:
- Place a serving of hot steamed rice in a bowl.
- Pour the hot green tea or dashi over the rice until it is almost submerged. The amount of liquid can be adjusted based on your preference for a soupy or drier consistency.

Add Toppings:
- Sprinkle your chosen toppings over the rice and tea. You can be creative and mix and match toppings according to your taste.

Season with Soy Sauce and Wasabi:

- Drizzle a bit of soy sauce over the toppings for added flavor. If you like a bit of heat, you can also add a small amount of wasabi.

Optional Nori Garnish:
- If desired, garnish with shredded nori seaweed on top.

Serve Immediately:
- Serve Ochazuke immediately while it's warm. The combination of flavors and textures creates a comforting and satisfying dish.

Ochazuke is a versatile dish that allows for personalization based on your taste preferences. It's a great way to use leftover rice and create a quick and delicious meal. Feel free to experiment with different toppings to suit your mood or the ingredients you have on hand.

Chicken Teriyaki Bowl

Ingredients:

For the Teriyaki Sauce:

- 1/2 cup soy sauce
- 1/4 cup mirin (sweet rice wine)
- 2 tablespoons sake (Japanese rice wine) or white wine
- 2 tablespoons sugar
- 1 teaspoon grated ginger
- 1 teaspoon minced garlic

For the Chicken:

- 1.5 lbs boneless, skinless chicken thighs, cut into bite-sized pieces
- Salt and pepper, to taste
- 2 tablespoons vegetable oil

For the Bowl:

- Steamed Japanese short-grain rice
- Sesame seeds, for garnish
- Sliced green onions, for garnish
- Steamed broccoli or other vegetables (optional)

Instructions:

For the Teriyaki Sauce:

    Combine Ingredients:
- In a small bowl, whisk together soy sauce, mirin, sake, sugar, grated ginger, and minced garlic. Ensure that the sugar is completely dissolved.

    Set Aside:
- Set aside the teriyaki sauce for later use.

For the Chicken:

    Season Chicken:
- Season the chicken pieces with salt and pepper.

    Cook Chicken:

- Heat vegetable oil in a large skillet or wok over medium-high heat. Add the seasoned chicken pieces and cook until browned and cooked through.

Add Teriyaki Sauce:
- Pour the prepared teriyaki sauce over the cooked chicken. Stir well to coat the chicken in the sauce.

Simmer:
- Allow the chicken and teriyaki sauce to simmer for a few minutes until the sauce thickens and glazes the chicken.

Assembling the Chicken Teriyaki Bowl:

Serve Over Rice:
- Spoon the teriyaki chicken over a bed of steamed Japanese short-grain rice in individual serving bowls.

Garnish:
- Garnish the Chicken Teriyaki Bowl with sesame seeds and sliced green onions.

Optional Vegetables:
- Add steamed broccoli or other vegetables on the side for added color and nutrition.

Serve Immediately:
- Serve the Chicken Teriyaki Bowl immediately, and enjoy the delicious combination of tender teriyaki chicken and fluffy rice.

This Chicken Teriyaki Bowl is a flavorful and satisfying meal that can be customized with your favorite vegetables or additional toppings. The homemade teriyaki sauce adds a perfect balance of sweetness and umami to the dish. It's a classic and popular choice in Japanese cuisine.

Hōrensō no Goma-ae (Spinach with Sesame Dressing)

Ingredients:

- 1 bunch of spinach, washed and trimmed
- 2 tablespoons sesame seeds
- 1 tablespoon soy sauce
- 1 tablespoon sugar
- 1 tablespoon mirin (sweet rice wine)
- 1 tablespoon sake (Japanese rice wine)

Instructions:

Blanch the Spinach:
- Bring a pot of water to a boil. Add a pinch of salt. Blanch the spinach in boiling water for about 1-2 minutes until just wilted.
- Quickly transfer the blanched spinach to a bowl of ice water to cool and stop the cooking process.
- Once cooled, squeeze excess water from the spinach and roughly chop it into bite-sized pieces.

Prepare Sesame Seeds:
- Toast the sesame seeds in a dry pan over medium heat until they become fragrant and lightly browned. Be careful not to burn them.
- Grind the toasted sesame seeds using a mortar and pestle or a grinder until you get a coarse powder.

Make the Sesame Dressing:
- In a small bowl, mix the ground sesame seeds with soy sauce, sugar, mirin, and sake. Stir well until the sugar is dissolved.

Combine Spinach and Sesame Dressing:
- Toss the chopped spinach with the sesame dressing, ensuring that the spinach is well coated.

Serve:
- Transfer the Hōrensō no Goma-ae to a serving dish.

Optional Garnish:
- If desired, you can sprinkle a few whole sesame seeds on top for garnish.

Serve Cold or at Room Temperature:
- Hōrensō no Goma-ae can be served immediately or refrigerated for a while before serving, allowing the flavors to meld.

Hōrensō no Goma-ae makes for a delightful side dish that complements the richness of sesame with the freshness of blanched spinach. It's a healthy and flavorful addition to your Japanese meal.

Kani Tamago Sushi (Crab and Egg Sushi)

Ingredients:

For the Tamago (Japanese Sweet Omelet):

- 4 large eggs
- 2 tablespoons sugar
- 2 tablespoons mirin (sweet rice wine)
- 2 tablespoons soy sauce
- Vegetable oil for cooking

For the Sushi Rice:

- 2 cups sushi rice
- 1/4 cup rice vinegar
- 2 tablespoons sugar
- 1 teaspoon salt

For the Filling:

- Imitation crab meat (kani kama), shredded
- Avocado, sliced (optional)
- Nori (seaweed) sheets, cut into half sheets
- Sesame seeds (optional, for garnish)

For Rolling:

- Bamboo sushi rolling mat
- Plastic wrap

Instructions:

For the Tamago (Japanese Sweet Omelet):

Prepare Tamago Mixture:
- In a bowl, whisk together eggs, sugar, mirin, and soy sauce until well combined.

Cook Tamago:
- Heat a non-stick frying pan over medium heat and lightly oil it. Pour a thin layer of the tamago mixture into the pan.
- Once the edges are set, roll the omelet towards you using chopsticks or a spatula to create a thin log. Push the rolled log to the far end of the pan.

- Add a little more of the tamago mixture to the empty part of the pan, lifting the rolled log slightly to let the new mixture flow underneath.
- Once the new layer sets, roll it onto the existing log. Repeat this process until all the tamago mixture is used.
- Remove the rolled tamago log from the pan and let it cool. Slice the tamago log into thin strips.

For the Sushi Rice:

Prepare Sushi Rice:

- Rinse the sushi rice under cold water until the water runs clear. Cook the rice according to the package instructions.
- While the rice is still hot, mix it with a mixture of rice vinegar, sugar, and salt. Allow the rice to cool to room temperature.

Assembling Kani Tamago Sushi:

Prepare Nori Sheets:
- Place a half-sheet of nori on the bamboo sushi rolling mat, shiny side down.

Spread Sushi Rice:
- Wet your hands and spread a thin layer of sushi rice over the nori, leaving about 1 inch at the top edge.

Add Filling:
- Arrange strips of tamago and shredded imitation crab meat (kani kama) along the center of the rice. Optionally, add slices of avocado.

Roll the Sushi:
- Using the bamboo rolling mat, start rolling the sushi from the bottom edge, tucking in the filling. Roll it tightly but gently.

Seal the Edge:
- Moisten the top edge of the nori sheet with a little water and press to seal the edge of the roll.

Slice the Roll:
- With a sharp, wet knife, slice the roll into bite-sized pieces.

Garnish (Optional):
- Sprinkle sesame seeds on top for garnish if desired.

Repeat:
- Repeat the process with the remaining ingredients.

Serve:
- Arrange the Kani Tamago Sushi on a plate and serve with soy sauce and pickled ginger.

Kani Tamago Sushi is a delightful combination of sweet tamago, savory crab meat, and creamy avocado if included. It's a great sushi option for those who prefer a milder and slightly sweet flavor profile. Enjoy these rolls as a snack, appetizer, or part of a sushi platter.

Ika Geso Karaage (Fried Squid Tentacles)

Ingredients:

- Squid tentacles (ika geso), cleaned
- Vegetable oil, for frying

For the Marinade:

- 2 tablespoons soy sauce
- 1 tablespoon sake (Japanese rice wine)
- 1 teaspoon ginger, grated
- 1 teaspoon garlic, minced

For the Karaage Batter:

- 1 cup all-purpose flour
- 2 tablespoons cornstarch
- 1/2 teaspoon baking powder
- 1 cup cold water
- Ice cubes

Instructions:

Clean the Squid Tentacles:
- If you have whole squid, separate the tentacles from the body. Clean and remove any remaining innards, beak, and cartilage. Rinse well under cold water.

Marinate the Tentacles:
- In a bowl, mix together soy sauce, sake, grated ginger, and minced garlic. Add the squid tentacles to the marinade, ensuring they are well-coated. Allow them to marinate for at least 15-30 minutes.

Prepare the Karaage Batter:
- In a separate bowl, whisk together all-purpose flour, cornstarch, baking powder, and cold water. Add ice cubes to keep the batter cold.

Heat the Oil:
- Heat vegetable oil in a deep fryer or a heavy-bottomed pan to 350-375°F (175-190°C).

Coat Squid in Batter:
- Dip each marinated squid tentacle into the karaage batter, ensuring they are fully coated.

Fry the Squid:
- Carefully place the battered squid tentacles into the hot oil. Fry in small batches to avoid overcrowding.
- Fry for 2-3 minutes or until the tentacles are golden brown and crispy.

Drain Excess Oil:
- Use a slotted spoon to remove the fried squid from the oil. Place them on a plate lined with paper towels to drain any excess oil.

Serve:
- Serve Ika Geso Karaage hot with a side of soy sauce, lemon wedges, or your favorite dipping sauce.

Ika Geso Karaage is a crunchy and flavorful snack that is perfect for sharing. The combination of the savory marinade and the light, crispy batter creates a delightful treat. Enjoy these fried squid tentacles as an appetizer or part of a Japanese-style meal.

Buta Kakuni (Braised Pork Belly)

Ingredients:

- 2 pounds (about 1 kg) pork belly, skin-on, cut into large cubes
- 1 cup dashi (Japanese soup stock)
- 1/2 cup soy sauce
- 1/2 cup sake (Japanese rice wine)
- 1/2 cup mirin (sweet rice wine)
- 1/4 cup sugar
- 4 cloves garlic, peeled and smashed
- 2-inch piece of ginger, sliced
- 2 green onions, cut into large pieces (white and green parts separated)
- 2 dried shiitake mushrooms (optional, for extra flavor)

Instructions:

Prepare the Pork Belly:
- Cut the pork belly into large cubes, about 2 inches in size.

Blanch the Pork:
- Bring a pot of water to a boil. Add the pork belly cubes and boil for 5-7 minutes to remove impurities. Drain and rinse the pork under cold water.

Simmering Broth:
- In a large pot or Dutch oven, combine dashi, soy sauce, sake, mirin, sugar, garlic, ginger, green onion whites, and dried shiitake mushrooms if using.

Add Pork Belly:
- Add the blanched pork belly to the pot, making sure it's submerged in the broth.

Simmering:
- Bring the broth to a simmer over medium heat. Once simmering, reduce the heat to low to maintain a gentle simmer.

Cover and Cook:
- Cover the pot with a lid slightly ajar and let the pork simmer for 2 to 2.5 hours, or until it becomes tender. Stir occasionally.

Check Doneness:
- Check the pork for tenderness by inserting a fork into a piece. It should be fork-tender and almost melt in your mouth.

Adjust Flavor:
- Adjust the seasoning if needed by adding more soy sauce, mirin, or sugar according to your taste.

Finish Cooking:
- Remove the dried shiitake mushrooms and discard. Continue simmering uncovered for an additional 15-30 minutes, allowing the sauce to thicken.

Serve:
- Serve the Buta Kakuni over steamed rice, garnished with green onion slices. Optionally, drizzle a bit of the braising liquid over the pork.

Buta Kakuni is a flavorful and comforting dish that is often enjoyed with a bowl of steamed rice. The slow braising process allows the pork belly to absorb the rich flavors of the broth, resulting in a tender and succulent dish.

Yaki Imo (Roasted Sweet Potatoes)

Ingredients:

- Sweet potatoes (Japanese sweet potatoes are commonly used, but any variety can be used)
- Aluminum foil

Instructions:

Choose Sweet Potatoes:
- Select sweet potatoes of your choice. Japanese sweet potatoes, such as Satsumaimo, are popular for Yaki Imo, but other varieties work well too.

Preheat Oven:
- Preheat your oven to 375°F (190°C).

Clean Sweet Potatoes:
- Wash and scrub the sweet potatoes thoroughly to remove any dirt. You can leave the skin on for a rustic touch.

Wrap in Aluminum Foil:
- Individually wrap each sweet potato in aluminum foil. This helps retain moisture and allows the potatoes to steam while roasting.

Bake in the Oven:
- Place the wrapped sweet potatoes directly on the oven rack or on a baking sheet.
- Bake for approximately 1 to 1.5 hours, or until the sweet potatoes are soft and easily pierced with a fork. The cooking time may vary depending on the size and type of sweet potatoes.

Rest and Serve:
- Once done, let the sweet potatoes rest for a few minutes before unwrapping. This allows them to continue cooking and develop a sweeter flavor.

Serve Warm:
- Serve the Yaki Imo warm. The skin should be crispy, and the inside should be soft and sweet.

Optional: Charcoal Grilling (Traditional Method):
- For a more traditional touch, you can mimic the charcoal-grilled flavor by using a gas stove. Carefully hold each wrapped sweet potato over an open flame, turning it to evenly char the skin.

Enjoy:

- Yaki Imo is often enjoyed as is, but you can also enhance the flavor by spreading a little butter on top or sprinkling a touch of salt.

Yaki Imo is not just a delicious treat; it also brings a warm and nostalgic feeling, especially during the colder months. The slow roasting process brings out the natural sweetness of the potatoes, making them a comforting and satisfying snack.

Atsuyaki Tamago (Thick Japanese Omelette)

Ingredients:

- 4 large eggs
- 2 tablespoons sugar
- 1 tablespoon mirin (sweet rice wine)
- 1 tablespoon soy sauce
- 1/2 teaspoon salt
- Vegetable oil for cooking

Equipment:

- Tamagoyaki pan (Japanese rectangular omelette pan)
- Bamboo sushi rolling mat

Instructions:

Prepare Tamagoyaki Pan:
- Heat the tamagoyaki pan over medium heat. Brush the inside of the pan with a thin layer of vegetable oil using a paper towel.

Mix the Egg Mixture:
- In a bowl, whisk together the eggs, sugar, mirin, soy sauce, and salt until well combined.

Cooking the First Layer:
- Pour a thin layer of the egg mixture into the tamagoyaki pan, just enough to cover the bottom. Allow it to set slightly but not completely.

Rolling the First Layer:
- Using chopsticks or a spatula, gently roll the cooked layer from one end to the other, pushing it to the opposite end of the pan.

Re-oil the Pan:
- Brush the empty part of the pan with a little more oil.

Pour the Second Layer:
- Pour another thin layer of the egg mixture into the pan, making sure it flows under the rolled egg.

Lift and Roll:
- Lift the rolled egg to let the new layer flow underneath. Roll the egg back over the new layer.

Repeat the Process:

- Repeat steps 5-7 until you have used all of the egg mixture. The layers should form a neat roll.

Shape the Tamago:
- Once the egg is fully cooked, shape it into a neat rectangular log by pressing it against one end of the pan using the bamboo sushi rolling mat.

Let It Cool:
- Allow the Atsuyaki Tamago to cool for a few minutes in the pan.

Slice and Serve:
- Carefully remove the rolled omelette from the pan. Slice it into bite-sized pieces with a sharp knife.

Serve Warm or at Room Temperature:
- Atsuyaki Tamago can be served warm or at room temperature. Enjoy it on its own or as part of a sushi platter.

Atsuyaki Tamago is a delightful combination of sweet and savory flavors and is a popular addition to bento boxes and sushi meals. With a little practice, you can achieve the characteristic layers and smooth texture that make this Japanese omelette so delicious.

Yuba Salad (Tofu Skin Salad)

Ingredients:

For the Salad:

- 1 package of yuba (dried tofu skin)
- Mixed salad greens (lettuce, spinach, arugula, etc.)
- Cherry tomatoes, halved
- Cucumber, thinly sliced
- Carrots, julienned
- Avocado, sliced
- Radishes, thinly sliced (optional)
- Sesame seeds, for garnish

For the Dressing:

- 2 tablespoons soy sauce
- 1 tablespoon rice vinegar
- 1 tablespoon mirin (sweet rice wine)
- 1 tablespoon sesame oil
- 1 teaspoon sugar
- 1 teaspoon grated ginger
- 1 clove garlic, minced

Instructions:

Prepare Yuba:
- If using dried yuba, rehydrate it according to the package instructions. This often involves soaking it in warm water until it becomes soft and pliable.

Slice Yuba:
- Once rehydrated, slice the yuba into thin strips or bite-sized pieces.

Prepare Salad Greens:
- Wash and prepare the mixed salad greens, cherry tomatoes, cucumber, carrots, avocado, and radishes.

Assemble Salad:
- In a large salad bowl, combine the salad greens, sliced yuba, cherry tomatoes, cucumber, carrots, avocado, and radishes.

Make the Dressing:

- In a small bowl, whisk together soy sauce, rice vinegar, mirin, sesame oil, sugar, grated ginger, and minced garlic. Adjust the seasoning according to your taste.

Dress the Salad:
- Pour the dressing over the salad and toss gently to coat everything evenly.

Garnish:
- Sprinkle sesame seeds on top for added texture and flavor.

Serve:
- Divide the Yuba Salad into individual serving plates or bowls. Serve immediately.

Yuba Salad is not only delicious but also offers a variety of textures and flavors. The yuba adds a unique chewy texture, while the fresh vegetables provide a crisp and vibrant contrast. The dressing enhances the overall taste with its savory, sweet, and slightly tangy notes. Enjoy this nutritious and satisfying salad as a light meal or a refreshing side dish.

Kakiage (Vegetable Tempura Fritters)

Ingredients:

For the Kakiage:

- 1 cup all-purpose flour
- 1 cup ice-cold water
- Assorted vegetables (onions, carrots, sweet potatoes, etc.), julienned
- Optional: Shrimp, peeled and deveined
- Vegetable oil for frying

For the Dipping Sauce:

- 1/4 cup soy sauce
- 2 tablespoons mirin (sweet rice wine)
- 1 tablespoon dashi (Japanese soup stock), or water
- 1 tablespoon sugar

Instructions:

For the Dipping Sauce:

Prepare Dipping Sauce:
- In a small saucepan, combine soy sauce, mirin, dashi or water, and sugar. Heat over low heat until the sugar dissolves. Remove from heat and let it cool.

For the Kakiage:

Prepare Vegetables:
- Julienne assorted vegetables into thin strips. If using shrimp, cut them into small pieces.

Make Tempura Batter:
- In a bowl, mix all-purpose flour and ice-cold water until just combined. It's okay if the batter is a bit lumpy. The key is to keep it cold.

Combine Vegetables and Batter:
- Add the julienned vegetables (and shrimp if using) to the tempura batter. Mix until the vegetables are well coated.

Heat Oil:
- Heat vegetable oil in a deep fryer or a deep pan to 350-375°F (175-190°C).

Fry Kakiage:

- Drop spoonfuls of the vegetable and batter mixture into the hot oil, creating small fritters. Fry until they are golden brown and crispy.

Drain Excess Oil:
- Use a slotted spoon to remove the kakiage from the oil. Place them on a plate lined with paper towels to drain excess oil.

Serve:
- Serve the kakiage immediately while they are hot and crispy. Enjoy them with the prepared dipping sauce.

Kakiage is often enjoyed as a snack, appetizer, or side dish. The combination of various vegetables and the light, crispy tempura batter creates a delightful texture and flavor. Dip the kakiage into the savory dipping sauce for an extra burst of taste. It's a delicious and popular dish in Japanese cuisine.

Sake and Ikura Don (Salmon and Salmon Roe Rice Bowl)

Ingredients:

- Sushi rice (cooked according to package instructions)
- Fresh salmon, thinly sliced
- Salmon roe (ikura)
- Soy sauce, for drizzling
- Wasabi, for serving
- Pickled ginger (gari), for serving
- Nori strips, for garnish (optional)
- Chopped green onions, for garnish (optional)
- Sesame seeds, for garnish (optional)

Instructions:

Prepare Sushi Rice:
- Cook sushi rice according to the package instructions. Allow it to cool slightly.

Assemble the Donburi Bowl:
- Place a serving of sushi rice in each bowl or on a plate.

Arrange Salmon Slices:
- Lay thinly sliced fresh salmon over the sushi rice in an attractive arrangement.

Add Salmon Roe:
- Gently spoon salmon roe (ikura) over the salmon slices. Be generous with the amount, as it adds a burst of flavor.

Drizzle with Soy Sauce:
- Drizzle a bit of soy sauce over the salmon and salmon roe for added seasoning. Adjust according to your taste.

Serve with Condiments:
- Serve the Sake and Ikura Don with small portions of wasabi, pickled ginger (gari), and any optional condiments like nori strips, chopped green onions, or sesame seeds.

Enjoy Immediately:
- Sake and Ikura Don is best enjoyed immediately while the salmon is fresh and the rice is still warm.

Optional Garnishes:
- If desired, garnish the bowl with nori strips, chopped green onions, or a sprinkle of sesame seeds for added visual appeal.

This Sake and Ikura Don is a luxurious and visually stunning dish that showcases the richness of fresh salmon and the delightful pop of salmon roe. It's a perfect way to indulge in the flavors of the sea over a bed of perfectly seasoned sushi rice. Customize the bowl with your favorite condiments and enjoy the elegant simplicity of this classic Japanese dish.

Hōtō Miso Soup

Ingredients:

For the Broth:

- 6 cups dashi (Japanese soup stock)
- 3 tablespoons white miso paste
- 2 tablespoons soy sauce
- 1 tablespoon mirin (sweet rice wine)

For the Soup:

- 200g hōtō noodles (or udon noodles as a substitute)
- 1 carrot, sliced
- 1 leek, sliced
- 1/2 kabocha squash, peeled and diced
- 1 onion, sliced
- 1 cup shiitake mushrooms, sliced
- 1 cup napa cabbage, chopped
- 1 cup spinach, chopped
- 1 block firm tofu, cut into cubes
- Salt and pepper, to taste

Optional Garnish:

- Green onions, chopped
- Sesame seeds
- Red pepper flakes

Instructions:

Prepare Dashi:
- In a pot, bring dashi to a simmer. Dashi can be made using bonito flakes, kombu (dried kelp), or a combination of both.

Add Vegetables:
- Add sliced carrot, leek, kabocha squash, onion, shiitake mushrooms, napa cabbage, and tofu to the simmering dashi. Cook until the vegetables are tender.

Cook Hōtō Noodles:
- In a separate pot, cook the hōtō noodles according to the package instructions. If using udon noodles, follow the instructions on the package.

Make Miso Broth:
- In a small bowl, mix white miso paste, soy sauce, and mirin. Take a ladle of hot broth from the soup pot and mix it into the miso paste until smooth.

- Add the miso mixture back into the soup pot and stir gently to combine. Be careful not to boil the miso, as it can lose its flavor.

Season and Adjust:
- Season the soup with salt and pepper to taste. Adjust the miso, soy sauce, or mirin if needed to achieve the desired flavor.

Add Spinach:
- Add chopped spinach to the soup just before serving. Stir until the spinach wilts.

Assemble:
- Divide the cooked hōtō noodles into bowls and ladle the hot miso soup over the noodles and vegetables.

Garnish (Optional):
- Garnish with chopped green onions, sesame seeds, or red pepper flakes for added flavor and visual appeal.

Serve Immediately:
- Hōtō Miso Soup is best enjoyed immediately while it's hot. Serve it as a comforting and nourishing meal.

Hōtō Miso Soup combines the rich umami flavors of miso with hearty vegetables and noodles, making it a satisfying and warming dish. It's a wonderful way to enjoy a comforting bowl of soup with a unique twist.

Hōtō Miso Soup

Ingredients:

For the Broth:

- 6 cups dashi (Japanese soup stock)
- 3 tablespoons white miso paste
- 2 tablespoons soy sauce
- 1 tablespoon mirin (sweet rice wine)

For the Soup:

- 200g hōtō noodles (or udon noodles as a substitute)
- 1 carrot, sliced
- 1 leek, sliced
- 1/2 kabocha squash, peeled and diced
- 1 onion, sliced
- 1 cup shiitake mushrooms, sliced
- 1 cup napa cabbage, chopped
- 1 cup spinach, chopped
- 1 block firm tofu, cut into cubes
- Salt and pepper, to taste

Optional Garnish:

- Green onions, chopped
- Sesame seeds
- Red pepper flakes

Instructions:

Prepare Dashi:
- In a pot, bring dashi to a simmer. Dashi can be made using bonito flakes, kombu (dried kelp), or a combination of both.

Add Vegetables:
- Add sliced carrot, leek, kabocha squash, onion, shiitake mushrooms, napa cabbage, and tofu to the simmering dashi. Cook until the vegetables are tender.

Cook Hōtō Noodles:
- In a separate pot, cook the hōtō noodles according to the package instructions. If using udon noodles, follow the instructions on the package.

Make Miso Broth:
- In a small bowl, mix white miso paste, soy sauce, and mirin. Take a ladle of hot broth from the soup pot and mix it into the miso paste until smooth.

- Add the miso mixture back into the soup pot and stir gently to combine. Be careful not to boil the miso, as it can lose its flavor.

Season and Adjust:
- Season the soup with salt and pepper to taste. Adjust the miso, soy sauce, or mirin if needed to achieve the desired flavor.

Add Spinach:
- Add chopped spinach to the soup just before serving. Stir until the spinach wilts.

Assemble:
- Divide the cooked hōtō noodles into bowls and ladle the hot miso soup over the noodles and vegetables.

Garnish (Optional):
- Garnish with chopped green onions, sesame seeds, or red pepper flakes for added flavor and visual appeal.

Serve Immediately:
- Hōtō Miso Soup is best enjoyed immediately while it's hot. Serve it as a comforting and nourishing meal.

Hōtō Miso Soup combines the rich umami flavors of miso with hearty vegetables and noodles, making it a satisfying and warming dish. It's a wonderful way to enjoy a comforting bowl of soup with a unique twist.

Tofu Scramble with Vegetables

Ingredients:

- 1 block firm or extra-firm tofu, pressed and crumbled
- 1 tablespoon oil (olive oil, canola oil, or your preferred cooking oil)
- 1 onion, diced
- 2 bell peppers, diced (any color)
- 1 cup cherry tomatoes, halved
- 2 cups fresh spinach or kale, chopped
- 2 cloves garlic, minced
- 1 teaspoon turmeric powder (for color)
- Salt and pepper, to taste
- Optional toppings: avocado, salsa, nutritional yeast, chopped herbs

Instructions:

Prepare Tofu:
- Press the tofu to remove excess water. Crumble it using your hands or a fork.

Sauté Vegetables:
- In a large skillet, heat oil over medium heat. Add diced onions and sauté until translucent.
- Add bell peppers and cook for a few minutes until they begin to soften.
- Stir in minced garlic and cook for an additional 30 seconds.

Add Tofu:
- Add the crumbled tofu to the skillet. Sprinkle turmeric powder over the tofu to give it a yellow color similar to scrambled eggs.

Season:
- Season the tofu and vegetables with salt and pepper. You can also add other spices like cumin, paprika, or nutritional yeast for extra flavor.

Cook and Stir:
- Cook the tofu and vegetables, stirring frequently, until the tofu is heated through and slightly golden. This usually takes about 8-10 minutes.

Add Tomatoes and Greens:
- Add halved cherry tomatoes and chopped spinach or kale to the skillet. Cook for an additional 2-3 minutes until the greens are wilted, and the tomatoes are softened.

Adjust Seasoning:

- Taste and adjust the seasoning if needed. You can add more salt, pepper, or spices according to your preference.

Serve:
- Remove the skillet from heat. Serve the tofu scramble hot, garnished with optional toppings like avocado slices, salsa, nutritional yeast, or chopped herbs.

Enjoy:
- Enjoy your tofu scramble with toast, in a wrap, or on its own. It's a versatile and satisfying plant-based breakfast or brunch option.

Feel free to get creative and add other vegetables, herbs, or spices to customize your tofu scramble to suit your taste preferences.

Okara Korokke (Soy Pulp Croquettes)

Ingredients:

For the Croquettes:

- 2 cups okara (soy pulp)
- 1 cup cooked and mashed potatoes
- 1 onion, finely chopped
- 1 carrot, grated
- 1/2 cup frozen peas, thawed
- 2 tablespoons soy sauce
- 1 tablespoon mirin (sweet rice wine)
- 1 tablespoon vegetable oil
- Salt and pepper, to taste
- Bread crumbs, for coating
- Vegetable oil, for frying

For the Dipping Sauce:

- 3 tablespoons soy sauce
- 2 tablespoons mirin
- 1 tablespoon water

Instructions:

Prepare Okara:
- If your okara is wet, gently squeeze out excess liquid using a cheesecloth or paper towels.

Mix Ingredients:
- In a large bowl, combine okara, mashed potatoes, chopped onion, grated carrot, thawed peas, soy sauce, mirin, vegetable oil, salt, and pepper. Mix well until all ingredients are evenly combined.

Shape Croquettes:
- Take a portion of the mixture and shape it into a flat, oval or round croquette. Repeat until all the mixture is used.

Coat with Bread Crumbs:
- Roll each croquette in bread crumbs, ensuring they are evenly coated.

Heat Oil:
- In a deep fryer or a deep pan, heat vegetable oil to around 350°F (175°C).

Fry Croquettes:

- Carefully place the coated croquettes in the hot oil and fry until they become golden brown and crispy. Fry in batches to avoid overcrowding.

Drain Excess Oil:
- Use a slotted spoon to remove the fried croquettes from the oil. Place them on a plate lined with paper towels to drain excess oil.

Prepare Dipping Sauce:
- In a small bowl, mix together soy sauce, mirin, and water to create the dipping sauce.

Serve:
- Serve the Okara Korokke hot with the dipping sauce on the side.

Okara Korokke makes a tasty and nutritious snack or side dish. The combination of okara, potatoes, and vegetables creates a delightful texture, while the crispy coating adds a satisfying crunch. Enjoy these croquettes as a delicious way to use soy pulp in your cooking.

Tori Nanban Soba (Chicken Nanban Noodles)

Ingredients:

For the Chicken Nanban:

- 2 boneless, skinless chicken breasts
- Salt and pepper, to taste
- Flour, for dredging
- 1-2 eggs, beaten
- Vegetable oil, for frying

For the Nanban Sauce:

- 3 tablespoons soy sauce
- 3 tablespoons rice vinegar
- 3 tablespoons sugar
- 1 tablespoon mirin
- 1 tablespoon sake
- 1/2 teaspoon grated ginger
- 1 clove garlic, minced

For the Soba Noodles:

- 200g soba noodles
- Green onions, chopped (for garnish)
- Red chili flakes (optional, for spice)

Instructions:

For the Chicken Nanban:

Prepare Chicken:
- Cut the chicken breasts into bite-sized pieces. Season with salt and pepper.

Dredge in Flour:
- Dredge the chicken pieces in flour, shaking off any excess.

Coat with Egg:
- Dip the floured chicken in beaten eggs, ensuring each piece is coated.

Fry Chicken:
- In a pan, heat vegetable oil over medium-high heat. Fry the chicken until golden brown and cooked through. Remove and place on a plate lined with paper towels to absorb excess oil.

For the Nanban Sauce:

- Make Nanban Sauce:
  - In a small saucepan, combine soy sauce, rice vinegar, sugar, mirin, sake, grated ginger, and minced garlic. Heat over medium heat until the sugar dissolves, and the sauce slightly thickens. Remove from heat.
- Coat Chicken with Sauce:
  - Pour the Nanban sauce over the fried chicken, ensuring each piece is coated. Let it marinate while preparing the soba noodles.

For the Soba Noodles:

- Cook Soba Noodles:
  - Cook the soba noodles according to the package instructions. Drain and rinse under cold water to cool.
- Assemble Dish:
  - Divide the cooked soba noodles among serving bowls. Top with the chicken pieces and a drizzle of the Nanban sauce.
- Garnish:
  - Garnish with chopped green onions and, if desired, red chili flakes for a bit of spice.
- Serve:
  - Serve Tori Nanban Soba immediately, allowing the flavors to meld together. Enjoy the crispy chicken and the sweet and sour sauce over the cold soba noodles.

Tori Nanban Soba is a delightful combination of textures and flavors, making it a satisfying and refreshing dish, especially in warmer weather. Adjust the spiciness and sweetness of the Nanban sauce according to your taste preferences.

Chikuzenni (Simmered Chicken and Vegetables)

Ingredients:

- 1 lb (450g) chicken thighs, boneless and skinless, cut into bite-sized pieces
- 1/2 cup soy sauce
- 1/4 cup mirin (sweet rice wine)
- 1/4 cup sake
- 1 tablespoon sugar
- 2 cups dashi (Japanese soup stock)
- 1 tablespoon vegetable oil
- 1 large carrot, peeled and sliced into thick rounds
- 1 daikon radish, peeled and sliced into thick rounds
- 1 sweet potato, peeled and cut into chunks
- 1/2 lotus root, peeled and sliced
- 1 konnyaku (konjac yam), sliced into rectangles
- 4 shiitake mushrooms, stems removed
- 1 cup bamboo shoots, sliced
- 1/2 cup gobo (burdock root), julienned
- 1 leek, cut into thick rounds
- 4-5 snow peas, ends trimmed
- 2 tablespoons toasted white sesame seeds (for garnish)

Instructions:

Prepare Ingredients:
- Cut the chicken thighs into bite-sized pieces. Prepare and cut all the vegetables as indicated.

Marinate Chicken:
- In a bowl, combine soy sauce, mirin, sake, and sugar. Add the chicken pieces and let them marinate for at least 15-30 minutes.

Simmer Chicken:
- In a large pot or deep pan, heat vegetable oil over medium heat. Add the marinated chicken and cook until browned.
- Pour in dashi, cover the pot, and bring it to a simmer. Reduce heat to low and let it simmer for about 10-15 minutes until the chicken is cooked through.

Add Vegetables:
- Add all the prepared vegetables to the pot. Arrange them neatly and submerge them in the simmering broth.

Continue Simmering:
- Continue to simmer, covered, for another 20-30 minutes or until the vegetables are tender and flavorful.

Adjust Seasoning:
- Adjust the seasoning if needed by adding more soy sauce, mirin, or sugar according to your taste.

Finish and Garnish:
- Add snow peas to the pot in the last few minutes of cooking, allowing them to remain vibrant green.
- Once everything is cooked through and flavorful, garnish with toasted sesame seeds.

Serve:
- Serve Chikuzenni in individual bowls, making sure to distribute a variety of vegetables and chicken in each serving.

Chikuzenni is a comforting and nutritious dish that beautifully showcases the flavors of seasonal vegetables and tender chicken simmered in a savory broth. Enjoy it as a main dish for celebrations or as a part of a special meal.

Kuzumochi (Japanese Arrowroot Starch Cake)

Ingredients:

For Kuzumochi:

- 1 cup kuzuko (arrowroot starch)
- 2 cups water
- 1/4 cup sugar
- Additional potato starch or cornstarch (for dusting)

For Kuromitsu (Black Sugar Syrup):

- 1/2 cup kokuto (Japanese black sugar)
- 1/4 cup water

For Kinako (Roasted Soybean Flour):

- 1/2 cup kinako (roasted soybean flour)

Instructions:

For Kuzumochi:

> Prepare Kuzuko Mixture:
> - In a bowl, mix the kuzuko with water until smooth. Make sure there are no lumps.
>
> Cook Kuzumochi Mixture:
> - In a saucepan, heat the kuzuko mixture over medium heat. Stir continuously until it thickens.
>
> Add Sugar:
> - Add sugar to the thickened kuzuko mixture and continue to stir until the sugar is fully dissolved.
>
> Pour into Mold:
> - Pour the mixture into a mold or a shallow tray lined with plastic wrap. Smooth the surface with a spatula.
>
> Chill:
> - Allow the kuzumochi to cool to room temperature, and then refrigerate until it sets completely (usually takes a few hours).
>
> Cut into Pieces:
> - Once the kuzumochi has set, remove it from the mold and cut it into bite-sized pieces. Dust the pieces with potato starch or cornstarch to prevent sticking.

For Kuromitsu (Black Sugar Syrup):

Prepare Kuromitsu:
- In a small saucepan, combine kokuto (Japanese black sugar) and water. Heat over low heat, stirring continuously until the sugar is completely dissolved.

Simmer:
- Simmer the mixture for a few minutes until it thickens slightly. Remove from heat and let it cool.

For Kinako (Roasted Soybean Flour):

Prepare Kinako:
- In a separate dry pan, lightly toast the kinako over medium heat until it becomes fragrant. Be careful not to burn it.

Assemble:
- Serve the chilled kuzumochi pieces with a drizzle of kuromitsu (black sugar syrup) and a sprinkle of kinako (roasted soybean flour).

Enjoy:
- Kuzumochi is ready to be enjoyed as a delightful and chewy Japanese dessert.

Kuzumochi is a refreshing and subtly sweet treat that is perfect for warmer weather. The combination of the chewy texture, sweet black sugar syrup, and nutty roasted soybean flour creates a delightful balance of flavors and textures.

Sōmen Salad with Ponzu Dressing

Ingredients:

For the Salad:

- 200g sōmen noodles
- 1 cucumber, julienned
- 1 carrot, julienned
- 1 red bell pepper, thinly sliced
- 1 cup shredded lettuce or mixed greens
- 1/4 cup chopped cilantro or parsley (optional)
- Sesame seeds, for garnish

For the Ponzu Dressing:

- 1/4 cup soy sauce
- 2 tablespoons mirin
- 2 tablespoons rice vinegar
- 2 tablespoons freshly squeezed citrus juice (lemon, lime, or a combination)
- 1 tablespoon grated daikon radish (optional)
- 1 teaspoon sugar
- 1 teaspoon sesame oil

Instructions:

Cook Sōmen Noodles:
- Cook the sōmen noodles according to the package instructions. Once cooked, rinse them under cold water to cool them quickly and prevent sticking.

Prepare Vegetables:
- Julienne the cucumber and carrot. Thinly slice the red bell pepper. Shred the lettuce or prepare mixed greens. Chop cilantro or parsley if using.

Make Ponzu Dressing:
- In a small bowl, whisk together soy sauce, mirin, rice vinegar, freshly squeezed citrus juice, grated daikon radish (if using), sugar, and sesame oil. Adjust the proportions to achieve the desired balance of sweet, salty, and tangy flavors.

Assemble Salad:

- In a large bowl, combine the cooked and cooled sōmen noodles with the julienned cucumber, carrot, sliced red bell pepper, shredded lettuce, and chopped cilantro or parsley.

Drizzle with Ponzu Dressing:
- Drizzle the ponzu dressing over the salad. Toss gently to ensure all ingredients are well-coated with the dressing.

Chill:
- Refrigerate the salad for at least 30 minutes to allow the flavors to meld and the noodles to absorb the dressing.

Garnish and Serve:
- Before serving, garnish the Sōmen Salad with sesame seeds. Optionally, add more herbs for freshness.

Enjoy:
- Serve the Sōmen Salad chilled and enjoy this light and flavorful dish.

Sōmen Salad with Ponzu Dressing is perfect for warm days or as a refreshing side dish.

The combination of the thin somen noodles, crisp vegetables, and the zesty ponzu dressing creates a delightful and satisfying salad.

Yuzu Cheesecake

Ingredients:

For the Crust:

- 1 1/2 cups graham cracker crumbs
- 1/4 cup melted butter
- 2 tablespoons sugar

For the Cheesecake Filling:

- 4 packages (32 ounces) cream cheese, softened
- 1 cup sugar
- 4 large eggs
- 1 cup sour cream
- 1/4 cup all-purpose flour
- 1 tablespoon vanilla extract
- Zest and juice of 2 yuzu fruits (or substitute with a combination of lemon and lime)

For the Yuzu Glaze (Optional):

- 1/2 cup yuzu juice
- 1/4 cup sugar
- 1 tablespoon cornstarch
- Water (to dissolve cornstarch)

Instructions:

For the Crust:

Preheat Oven:
- Preheat your oven to 325°F (163°C).

Prepare Crust:
- In a bowl, mix graham cracker crumbs, melted butter, and sugar until well combined.

Press into Pan:
- Press the crumb mixture into the bottom of a 9-inch (23 cm) springform pan to form the crust.

Bake:
- Bake the crust in the preheated oven for about 10 minutes. Remove and allow it to cool while preparing the filling.

For the Cheesecake Filling:

- Lower Oven Temperature:
  - Reduce the oven temperature to 300°F (149°C).
- Prepare Filling:
  - In a large mixing bowl, beat the cream cheese until smooth. Add sugar and continue to beat until well combined.
- Add Eggs:
  - Add the eggs one at a time, mixing well after each addition.
- Incorporate Sour Cream, Flour, and Flavorings:
  - Mix in the sour cream, all-purpose flour, vanilla extract, yuzu zest, and yuzu juice. Ensure that the batter is smooth and well combined.
- Pour Over Crust:
  - Pour the cheesecake batter over the prepared crust in the springform pan.
- Bake:
  - Bake in the preheated oven for about 60-70 minutes or until the edges are set, and the center is slightly jiggly.
- Cool and Refrigerate:
  - Allow the cheesecake to cool in the oven with the door ajar for about an hour. Refrigerate for several hours or overnight to set completely.

For the Yuzu Glaze (Optional):

- Make Glaze:
  - In a small saucepan, combine yuzu juice, sugar, and cornstarch. Mix well.
- Heat and Thicken:
  - Heat the mixture over medium heat, stirring constantly until it thickens. If needed, dissolve additional cornstarch in water and add to achieve the desired thickness.
- Cool:
  - Allow the yuzu glaze to cool.
- Drizzle Over Cheesecake:
  - Before serving, drizzle the cooled yuzu glaze over the chilled cheesecake.
- Slice and Serve:
  - Slice the Yuzu Cheesecake and serve chilled.

Enjoy the delightful combination of creamy cheesecake and the unique citrusy flavor of yuzu in this refreshing dessert!

Katsudon (Pork Cutlet and Egg Rice Bowl)

Ingredients:

- 4 pork loin or pork tenderloin cutlets (tonkatsu)
- Salt and pepper, to taste
- Flour, for dusting
- 1-2 eggs, beaten
- Panko breadcrumbs, for coating
- Vegetable oil, for frying
- 1 onion, thinly sliced
- 1/4 cup soy sauce
- 2 tablespoons mirin (sweet rice wine)
- 2 tablespoons sake
- 1 tablespoon sugar
- 1 cup dashi (Japanese soup stock) or chicken broth
- 4 servings of cooked Japanese rice
- Green onions, chopped (for garnish)
- Nori (seaweed), thinly sliced (optional)

Instructions:

Prepare Tonkatsu:
- Season the pork cutlets with salt and pepper. Dust each cutlet with flour, dip in beaten eggs, and coat with Panko breadcrumbs.

Fry Tonkatsu:
- Heat vegetable oil in a pan over medium heat. Fry the pork cutlets until they are golden brown and cooked through. Place them on a paper towel to absorb excess oil, then slice them into strips.

Make Katsudon Sauce:
- In the same pan, remove any excess oil, leaving about 1 tablespoon. Add sliced onions and cook until they become translucent.
- In a bowl, mix soy sauce, mirin, sake, sugar, and dashi (or chicken broth). Pour this mixture into the pan with the onions. Bring it to a simmer.

Add Tonkatsu and Eggs:
- Place the sliced tonkatsu into the simmering sauce. Beat the remaining eggs and pour them over the tonkatsu.

Simmer:
- Cover the pan and simmer for a few minutes until the eggs are cooked to your liking.

Assemble Katsudon:
- Place a serving of cooked rice in a bowl. Spoon the tonkatsu and egg mixture over the rice.

Garnish:
- Garnish with chopped green onions and sliced nori if desired.

Serve:
- Serve the Katsudon hot, and enjoy the combination of crispy tonkatsu, savory sauce, and fluffy eggs over rice.

Katsudon is a comforting and flavorful dish that's easy to prepare at home. It's a great way to enjoy the classic combination of pork cutlet, eggs, and rice in a single bowl.

Kappa Maki (Cucumber Sushi Roll)

Ingredients:

- 2 sheets of nori (seaweed)
- 2 cups sushi rice, seasoned with rice vinegar, sugar, and salt
- 1/2 English cucumber, julienned into thin strips
- Soy sauce, for dipping (optional)
- Pickled ginger and wasabi, for serving (optional)

Instructions:

Prepare Sushi Rice:
- Cook sushi rice according to package instructions. Once cooked, season the rice with a mixture of rice vinegar, sugar, and salt. Allow the rice to cool to room temperature.

Prepare Cucumber:
- Julienne the cucumber into thin strips. It's recommended to remove the seeds from the cucumber to prevent excess moisture in the roll.

Prepare Nori Sheets:
- Place a bamboo sushi rolling mat on a flat surface. Put a sheet of plastic wrap on top of the mat. Lay a sheet of nori, shiny side down, on the plastic wrap.

Spread Sushi Rice:
- Wet your hands with water to prevent sticking, and spread a thin layer of sushi rice over the nori, leaving about half an inch at the top edge.

Add Cucumber Strips:
- Place a line of julienned cucumber strips along the bottom edge of the rice.

Roll the Sushi:
- Lift the edge of the bamboo mat closest to you with both hands, and begin rolling the nori and rice over the cucumber. Use the bamboo mat to shape the roll tightly.

Seal the Edge:
- Moisten the top edge of the nori with a little water to help seal the roll.

Slice the Roll:
- Using a sharp knife dipped in water, slice the roll into bite-sized pieces. Wipe the knife between cuts to keep the edges clean.

Repeat:
- Repeat the process with the remaining nori sheet and ingredients.

Serve:
- Arrange the Kappa Maki on a plate. Optionally, serve with soy sauce, pickled ginger, and wasabi for dipping.
Enjoy:
- Enjoy your homemade Kappa Maki as a light and refreshing sushi option.

Kappa Maki is a classic and simple sushi roll that showcases the clean and crisp taste of cucumber. It's perfect for those who prefer a vegetarian sushi option or enjoy a lighter sushi experience.

Saba Misoni (Mackerel Simmered in Miso)

Ingredients:

- 2 mackerel fillets, fresh or frozen (saba)
- 2 tablespoons vegetable oil
- 1 onion, thinly sliced
- 2 carrots, julienned
- 1/4 cup sake
- 2 tablespoons mirin
- 3 tablespoons sugar
- 1/3 cup miso paste (white or red miso)
- 1 cup dashi (Japanese soup stock) or water
- Green onions, chopped (for garnish)

Instructions:

Prepare Mackerel Fillets:
- If using frozen mackerel fillets, thaw them in the refrigerator overnight. Pat the fillets dry with paper towels.

Sear Mackerel:
- In a large pan, heat vegetable oil over medium-high heat. Sear the mackerel fillets on both sides until they are golden brown. Set aside.

Sauté Vegetables:
- In the same pan, add sliced onions and julienned carrots. Sauté until the vegetables are slightly softened.

Deglaze with Sake:
- Pour sake over the vegetables to deglaze the pan, scraping up any browned bits from the bottom.

Add Mirin and Sugar:
- Add mirin and sugar to the pan. Stir well until the sugar is dissolved.

Dissolve Miso:
- In a small bowl, mix miso paste with a small amount of dashi or water to create a smooth paste. Add the miso paste to the pan, stirring continuously to dissolve it into the liquid.

Pour Dashi (or Water):
- Gradually add the remaining dashi (or water) to the pan, stirring to combine all the ingredients.

Simmer Mackerel:

- Return the seared mackerel fillets to the pan. Bring the mixture to a gentle simmer.

Simmer Until Cooked:
- Cover the pan and simmer for about 15-20 minutes or until the mackerel is fully cooked and the flavors have melded.

Garnish and Serve:
- Garnish with chopped green onions before serving.

Serve Over Rice:
- Serve Saba Misoni over steamed rice, allowing the delicious miso sauce to coat the mackerel and infuse the rice with flavor.

Enjoy:
- Enjoy the savory and umami-rich flavors of Saba Misoni as a comforting Japanese dish.

Saba Misoni is a wonderful way to enjoy the bold taste of mackerel in a savory miso-based sauce. The combination of miso, sake, and mirin creates a delicious glaze that enhances the natural flavors of the fish. Serve it with rice for a satisfying meal.

Daikon Radish Salad with Shiso Dressing

Ingredients:

For the Salad:

- 1 medium daikon radish, peeled and julienned
- 1 carrot, peeled and julienned
- 1/4 cup chopped shiso leaves (fresh or pickled)
- 1 tablespoon toasted sesame seeds (for garnish)

For the Shiso Dressing:

- 3 tablespoons rice vinegar
- 2 tablespoons soy sauce
- 1 tablespoon mirin
- 1 tablespoon sesame oil
- 1 tablespoon sugar
- 1 teaspoon grated ginger
- 1 teaspoon grated garlic

Instructions:

For the Salad:

Prepare Daikon and Carrot:
- Peel the daikon radish and carrot. Julienne both vegetables into thin strips.

Chop Shiso Leaves:
- If using fresh shiso leaves, chop them finely. If using pickled shiso leaves, ensure they are drained and chopped.

Combine Vegetables:
- In a large bowl, combine the julienned daikon radish, carrot, and chopped shiso leaves.

For the Shiso Dressing:

Prepare Dressing:
- In a small bowl, whisk together rice vinegar, soy sauce, mirin, sesame oil, sugar, grated ginger, and grated garlic. Mix until the sugar is fully dissolved.

Toss Salad with Dressing:
- Pour the shiso dressing over the daikon and carrot mixture. Toss the salad gently to ensure the vegetables are evenly coated with the dressing.

Chill:
- Refrigerate the salad for at least 15-30 minutes to allow the flavors to meld and the vegetables to marinate.

Garnish:
- Before serving, sprinkle toasted sesame seeds over the salad as a garnish.

Serve:
- Serve Daikon Radish Salad with Shiso Dressing as a refreshing side dish or a light appetizer.

This salad showcases the crispness of daikon radish, the sweetness of carrots, and the aromatic notes of shiso, all complemented by the savory and slightly sweet shiso dressing. It makes a wonderful addition to a Japanese meal or as a light and refreshing salad on its own.

Chazuke (Green Tea Rice Soup)

Ingredients:

- Cooked Japanese rice (1 cup per serving)
- Hot green tea or dashi broth (about 1 cup per serving)
- Toppings of your choice (see suggestions below)
- Soy sauce, to taste
- Wasabi, to taste (optional)
- Nori (seaweed) strips, for garnish

Topping Suggestions:

Umeboshi (pickled plum): Pit and chop into small pieces.
Salmon: Grilled or smoked salmon flakes.
Tsukemono (pickled vegetables): Sliced or shredded pickled vegetables, such as takuan (pickled daikon) or cucumber.
Sesame Seeds: Toasted sesame seeds for added flavor.
Shredded Nori: Seaweed strips for a savory touch.
Chopped Scallions: Fresh green onions for a mild onion flavor.
Furikake: Japanese rice seasoning for added flavor.

Instructions:

Prepare Rice:
- Cook Japanese rice according to package instructions or using your preferred method.

Place Rice in Bowls:
- Scoop a serving of cooked rice into individual serving bowls.

Add Toppings:
- Arrange your chosen toppings over the rice. You can use a combination of different toppings for variety.

Pour Green Tea or Dashi:
- Heat green tea or dashi broth. Pour the hot liquid over the rice and toppings in each bowl.

Season:
- Add soy sauce to taste. If you enjoy some heat, you can also add a bit of wasabi.

Garnish:
- Garnish with nori strips and additional sesame seeds if desired.

Serve Immediately:
- Serve Chazuke while it's warm. The hot liquid will create a comforting and flavorful broth as it mixes with the rice and toppings.

Chazuke is a versatile dish that allows you to get creative with toppings, making it a comforting and customizable meal. It's a popular choice for a light and soothing meal, especially during colder weather.

www.ingramcontent.com/pod-product-compliance
Lightning Source LLC
LaVergne TN
LVHW061938070526
838199LV00060B/3868